IN HONOUR

"I WANT TO HONOUR THE INCREDIBLE, SELFLESS ORGAN DONOR WHO GAVE ME A SECOND CHANCE AT LIFE"

I dedicate the second edition of this book to a man I never got a chance to meet in this life. I do not know his name and I do not know where he comes from. On the 28th of February 2012 this man passed away in the ICU (Intensive Care Unit) in a hospital somewhere in Australia or New Zealand. Before this incredible man passed away, he made a decision to donate his organs to save the lives of others. At that time I was on my death bed and unable to breathe. I had been diagnosed with Terminal Idiopathic Pulmonary Fibrosis, which is a Lung Disease caused by your own immune system attacking you and as yet it has no cure. The only option is a Double Lung Transplant and I was very privileged to have been accepted onto the St Vincent's Hospital in Sydney, Australia's Transplant waiting list.

That night I got the call from the hospital to come in for my double lung transplant. Words cannot express the honour and joy I feel. In a letter, which is sent by the hospital without the donor family knowing me or me knowing them, I promised my incredible donor's family that I would not waste one breath with my second chance at life. You would not be reading this book if this man had not died and gave me new life. This book is titled THE KEY TO LIFE and it is all about you the reader and the incredible destiny that awaits you.

Thank you eternally my incredible donor and your family!!

Nigel

TESTIMONY FROM PASTOR TIM HALL
Evangelist & Founding Pastor, "Lifepoint Church" Adelaide, Australia

"THE KEY TO LIFE is a book that will inspire, challenge and astound you. It will open the mysteries of this life and the life to come by showing you that there are 2 births but 1 author in a most unique way. A must read book!" Pastor Tim Hall

Tim Hall is one of the greatest Evangelists in the world today, often preaching to crowds in excess of 100,000 people. Tim met THE KEY TO LIFE in 1974 at the age of 26, when he was an alcoholic High School Teacher and a Bohemian Artist. His life was turned upside down and he was radically healed and transformed by this experience. Not only is he an incredible Evangelist, but the funniest man on the planet and together with his awesome wife Jacque they are also the most giving and generous people I have ever met. He is also a gifted artist and his paintings blow my mind, (how come God gave him all the gifts)? Tim has written an incredible book entitled "Giant Killers", and let me assure you he knows what it's like fight the Giants that we all face in life. Invest in his book because it will transform your life. Tim to date has led more than 1,000,000 people to THE KEY TO LIFE and he is only just beginning.

You can contact Tim by visiting his website
www.timhall.com.au

TESTIMONY FROM FRED AH KUOI
Captain & Vice Captain, New Zealand Kiwis, Rugby League Team, 1979 - 1984.

Nigel Allan empowered and led by the Holy Spirit of the living God, has truly given us an amazing spiritual insight of God's creative power, through the natural occurrences of daily life. The detail and depth of his research into physical and natural evidence leaves one in awe that there is a God, and He has an amazing plan for each and every one of us. THE KEY TO LIFE will transform your thinking and challenge you to seek out the uniqueness that God has placed inside you to discover. Dare yourself to be transformed!
Fred Ah Kuoi

Fred Ah Kuoi, his beautiful wife Margot and their awesome 3 children moved to the USA in 1999 so that Fred and Margot could attend discipleship training in the Gospel. Fred Pastors a program that transforms lives using physical training and discipleship that presents the truth of what God says about our bodies and the vision that God has for them. Fred is a Pastor at Phoenix First Assembly, a Mega Church of some 6,000 people, which is connected to The Dream Centre in Phoenix and has other Centres in the USA. Its incredible programs are responsible for transforming the lives of thousands and thousands of ex prisoners, prostitutes and other lost and broken people from all walks of life. The people who attend the Dream Centre join a 6 month program which changes their lives from being broken to being made whole. I have had the honour of attending a graduation ceremony where I heard the stories of the people who completed and graduated from this program. I was in convulsive tears as I heard and saw how these beautiful people were healed and delivered from all the pain and sorrow that life had thrown at them. Fred Ah Kuoi is the same humble incredible leader now just as he was when leading the New Zealand Kiwis and is available for speaking and preaching engagements globally, and so I encourage you to contact him as he will bring transformation and increase to your company, sporting team, church or any other individual or organisation.

Contact Fred at this email address fredandmargot@gmail.com

TESTIMONY FROM PASTOR JURGEN MATTHESIUS
Lead Pastor, C3 Church San Diego

"This is one of those books where, as you are reading it you say to yourself, 'Oh my goodness, I can think of at least 10 people I know who should read this book. Nigel's research and presentation in this book make it an easy and enjoyable read, but simultaneously, powerfully, impacts your soul."

"I phoned Nigel one day after I had given one of his books to a young lady who had attempted suicide three times, and was threatening to try again. Three days after receiving the book she rang me and said 'Pastor Jurgen, thank you so much for the book! Now I do not want to commit suicide any more because I know that I am not a mistake and that I have value.'"

Pastor Jurgen Matthesius

TESTIMONY FROM PETER IRVINE
Author, Speaker and Co-Founder of Gloria Jean's Coffee's International

"I have just finished reading your book on my trip to the USA. It was a great and challenging read. Anyone reading this book will certainly be challenged."

*"You were created
on purpose,
for a purpose."*

The Key To Life by Nigel Allan
Published by w
Email: tktl@nigelallan.com
Web: www.nigelallan.com

Cover Art and Layout by Velvet Creative (velvet.com.au)

This book or parts thereof may not be reproduced in any form, stored in a retrieval system, or transmitted in any form by any means - electronic, mechanical, photocopy, recording, or otherwise - without prior written permission of the publisher, except as provided by Australian copyright law. Portions of or this entire book may appear on copyright cassette, compact disc, video, DVD and in other forms of multi-media presentations, invented or to be invented. Information in this book is in no way intended to replace independent professional opinion or advice. The author may not be held responsible for any action or claim resulting in the use or accuracy of any or all of the information contained in this book.

Scripture taken from the New King Version James Version. Copyright © 1979, 1980, 1982. By Thomas Nelson, Inc. Used by permission. All rights reserved.

Scripture taken from the New International Version. Copyright © 1973, 1978, 1984 International Bible Society. Used by permission of Zondervan. All rights reserved.

Scripture taken from the Amplified Bible, Copyright © 1954, 1958, 1962, 1964, 1965, 1987 by The Lockman Foundation. Used by permission. All rights reserved.

All other scripture quotations are taken from The King James Version. Public Domain.

Words in capitals, in bold or in scripture quotations are the emphasis of the author. The words "him", "his", "he", or "man" are sometimes used generically to describe people of both genders.

Some scientific and the evolution material sourced from The Seal Of God, by F.C. Payne (ISBN 0 908208 05 7) Revised and rewritten by E.R. FINCK in 1995. Legally deposited under the South Australian State Act February 20 1996 and National Library Canberra

Copyright © 2004 by Nigel Allan - The Publisher. All Rights Reserved.

International Standard Book No (ISBN) 0 646 42819 5

10 9 8 7 6 5 4 3

THE KEY TO LIFE

BORN A WINNER ◆ LIVE A WINNER ◆ DIE A WINNER

UNLOCK THE SECRETS TO YOUR SUCCESS
WITH THE KEY TO LIFE!

NIGEL ALLAN

DEDICATED TO

To my beautiful wife Lucy, my incredible children Bridget, Joshua and Zoe, thank you for allowing me to write this book at some of the most inconvenient times to you all. I love you all so much and thank you for trusting me with your lives.

From left to right, our beautiful daughter Bridget, our gorgeous granddaughter Indi, awesome son in law Lachlan, my stunning wife and rib Lucy, myself, our beautiful daughter Zoe and incredible son Joshua.

A VERY SPECIAL THANK YOU:

Warren & Tina O'Connor

To my best friend Warren O'Connor, you are such an intense and focussed man. Not only did you lead me to Jesus "THE KEY TO LIFE", but you displayed such compassion to me during one of the darkest periods of my life. You would drop everything time and time again to be at my side when I needed wisdom, focus and encouragement. I thank you Warren for leading me to Jesus who is not only THE KEY TO LIFE but is the AUTHOR OF LIFE. Me and my family love you, your beautiful wife Tina and your boys, Daniel, James and Jonathon.

CONTENTS

Acknowledgements	iii
Preface	v

PART ONE – Born A Winner

Chapter 1: You Can't Argue With The Facts	3
Chapter 2: You Can't Have Creation Without A Creator	17
Chapter 3: They're Off And Racing	23

PART TWO – Live A Winner

Chapter 4: The Long Arm Of The Law	39
Chapter 5: Words Are Your Best Friend Or Your Worst Enemy	71
Chapter 6: Get A Vision And See It To Fruition	87

PART THREE – Die A Winner

Chapter 7: Enough Of The Monkey Business	117
Chapter 8: The Proof Of The Pudding Is In The Eating	141
Chapter 9: Born Once, Die A Loser Born Twice, Die A Winner	179

About the Author	223

ACKNOWLEDGEMENTS

F.C. Payne and E.R. Finck your combined tireless work over many, many years has and will keep changing the lives of millions of people. Your incredible book THE SEAL OF GOD introduced me to THE KEY TO LIFE and to THE LIVING GOD. A friend gave it to me and as I lay in my bed reading it one night, I was unable to put it down until every single word was finished. I wept and wept as I read page after page of the awesome miracle of God's creation. At that time I was a lonely broken mess and now I pray my book will also impact millions of lives. Thank you so much!

I would like to thank Kenneth and Gloria Copeland not only for your invaluable information about Salvation and the Baptism in the Holy Spirit used in this book, but for your ministry that has changed the lives of millions of people around the world and empowered them to be winners.

ACKNOWLEDGEMENTS

I would also like to thank Mr. Tao (Andrew) Peng (Mathematician), for setting aside the time to work out the mathematical calculations of the sperm cell. We understand that these are not necessarily 100% accurate however they are only there to give you the reader a very clear understanding that you were BORN A WINNER.

I would like to thank Nathan Rigaud CFII for his effort in compiling the "Checklist for the Velocity Aircraft" as published in Velocity Views Newsletter Volume 33.

Chris you are an incredible inspiration to me and I love you my awesome friend. Thank you for the material about the things we need to remember. You are about to reap all that you have sown into my life.

PREFACE

Just before you read this Preface, I want to ask you to please stay with me because right now I am going to share with you from the depths of my heart. I am aware that if you do not yet know THE KEY TO LIFE, you may think my story about how this book was birthed is crazy, however it is the absolute truth, and I want to share it with you in order to lay a foundation for the rest of the book.

By now you have probably read the testimonies from the men on the covers, well these men and billions of other men, women and children right down through the ages have had their lives transformed and yours can be to.

This book was birthed during a 6pm service at our Church, C3 in Oxford Falls, in Sydney, Australia, at what we call altar call time. After every service when the preacher has finished the sermon he or

ACKNOWLEDGEMENTS

she gives and invitation for those people who do not yet have a relationship with THE KEY TO LIFE, to come down to the altar and to pray a simple prayer that invites Him to be their Lord and Saviour. For some reason whenever we were in Church, which was almost every service, when it came to altar call time, I was prompted very often when the invitation was being made to walk around the auditorium and the Holy Spirit would show me the people who wanted to come to the altar, but were just struggling a little to make that decision, and so I would quietly walk up to them and encourage them that to come to the altar would be the greatest decision of their lives, and if they wanted me to walk down with them I was very happy to do so, and most often that's what would happen.

Well, one night our Senior Pastor and Founder of C3 Churches, Pastor (Doctor) Phil Pringle was preaching and after finishing, he invited people to meet THE KEY TO LIFE. Many people came to the front, however Pastor Phil sensed there was one more person and so he waited, it seemed like an eternity, but because he is so sensitive to people he did not want this person to miss this incredible life changing opportunity. This particular night I did not sense to walk around until right then, and when he said the following words my heart started to race and I just knew something amazing was about to happen. Pastor Phil said, "There is a young man here and God has called you to preach the Gospel to the nation's of the world, however firstly you must be born again, (that means to meet THE KEY TO LIFE). He did not come forward and so, as I turned around, with my heart almost jumping out of my chest I looked up the back of the auditorium amongst the 1500 - 2000 people that were there that night and my eyes focussed on a young man of about 25 years of age. I left my seat and went up to him and said, you know he is talking about you don't you! He said to me "I'll be right mate" and I said, is your heart racing like mine, and he said

THE KEY TO LIFE

"yes it is" so I said why don't you come down with me and let God touch your life, and with tears in his eyes he said "alright let's go".

When we got to the front Pastor Phil said to him, "you are that man I was talking about", and as Pastor Phil said that I broke into tears and felt like I had just given birth. That night I lay on my bed and asked God to tell me what that was all about, I said what is this born again thing Lord and why do you get me walking around and helping people to go down to the altar. The Lord said to me, "Son you are a midwife" "I said I beg your pardon Lord what do you mean a midwife"? He said "just as a midwife helps children to be born in the natural, you help children be Born ……. Again, in the spiritual (spiritual birth). (We need to have 2 births 1 in the natural and 1 in the spiritual, as you will read about later in this book.) Then for the next 3 hours as I lay on my bed weeping, the contents of this book were birthed as the Lord opened up His incredible creation and salvation plan to me.

Well that's the truth hope you didn't mind me telling you how it really happened. I have had to apply this book to my own life over the last 3 years, since I was diagnosed with Pulmonary Fibrosis, then told I had a year to live without a double lung transplant, I lived through the darkest period of my life, claiming all that is in this book, got my double lung transplant a year ago, how honoured, privileged and thankful I am to the transplant medical team at St Vincent's hospital in Sydney, and to my incredible donor and his beautiful family. I learned from and incredible woman of God,

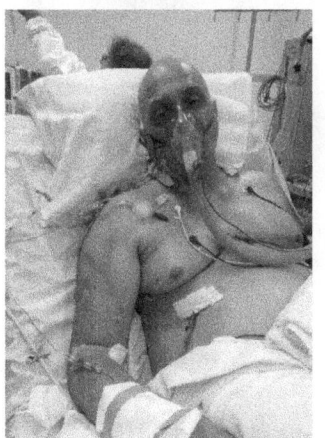
Me in the ICU after my Double Lung Transplant

vii

ACKNOWLEDGEMENTS

Lisa Bevere as she said "what you write on you will be tested on" and have I been tried and tested, but the great news is, this book worked for me and it will work for you, so please invest in your destiny, read it from cover to cover, not for me, but for you.

Regards - Nigel

PART ONE – BORN A WINNER

CHAPTER ONE
YOU CAN'T ARGUE WITH THE FACTS

Before we can begin this incredible journey together, we need to lay a foundation of truth and understanding about some irrefutable facts that will allow you to see into the unseen world and discover that you are a created miracle that did not just sort of happen.

THE FACTS

- Half of the necessary information required to make you came from your father's seed (sperm cell) and the other half came from your mother's seed (egg cell).

- There are normally 46 chromosomes that make up a human being, twenty-three came from your mother and twenty-three came from your father, a chromosome contains the genetic information that is required to create you.

- The information was genetically exclusive to that egg and that sperm that made you and it will never be duplicated in the creation of another human, in other words if a different sperm to the one that made you had joined with your mother's egg, it would not have been you, but someone else. The same would have applied if the sperm that made you joined with a different egg than the one that made you. Not all sperm are the same and not all eggs are the same, each has their own unique genetically designed code and this code is locked and we will not be given the combination to unlock it.

- Your parents had absolutely nothing to do with the design of your genetic information as it was written and designed without their approval or input and placed into their individual genes before they were created from their parent's seeds. Your parent's only input was to carry this information in their reproductive systems and then sow it at the appropriate time.

- You were not given a menu before you were born so that you could choose your height, your sex, your skin colour, or your personality.

- When the sperm cell meets the egg cell, the two become one and not the two become two.

- The human embryo becomes only a single cell when the two meet and then they divide at an incredible rate to end up as billions of cells.

- Marriage is about a man and a woman becoming one and this

same marriage takes place when the sperm of the man and the egg of the woman unite, they become one and in your case that marriage created you.

- Normally between 80 million and 800 million sperm are released by the male when a man and a woman unite together, yet only one single sperm is required to fertilise an egg.

- It is incredible to think that the number of sperm cells released can be on some occasions double or even triple the entire population of the USA (which is around 250,000,000) and what is more awesome is that you and I both won our race against the millions and millions of other competitors, then survived further unbelievable odds to be born.

- Your mother was born with around 1,000,000 egg cells in her ovary and yet in her entire life only around 400 would be released for a chance to be impregnated.

- One of these 400 egg cells out of the 1,000,000 was you and not only that, but you were released at a perfect time in history, because you had to meet the sperm cell that helped create you within a 36 hour fertilisation period or there would have been no you.

- Only recently have we been educated about DNA, yet this incredible substance was in the nucleus of the human cell from the beginning of human creation. This just magnifies the fact that we know very little about our incredible design.

- DNA (deoxyribonucleic acid) is the substance in the nucleus that enables the cells to reproduce and transmit <u>same species</u> characteristics from generation to generation.

YOU CAN'T ARGUE WITH THE FACTS

When we go to the local video store to hire out a video we are given a copy of the original, but are never given the actual original master. The epic movie 'The Ten Commandments' was set in Bible times around two thousand years ago and since the movie was first created, millions of copies of the original movie have been produced and sent to video stores all around the world.

Its creator wrote the DNA of this movie into the script and each time the original movie was copied it would only ever reproduce and transmit the exact same characteristics as the master, from generation to generation, to generation, to generation, to generation.

You could sit and watch this movie for the next 10 billion years and it will never turn into Star Wars, because it will only reproduce the same species.

Turning into Star Wars that is a ridiculous notion isn't it, well it can't be that ridiculous because there are millions of people who have been sold the lie that you and I were once a piece of green slime that crawled out of an ocean and then after thousands of generations, or billions of years of being a piece of slime, or maybe part fish and part mongoose, or part monkey and part dinosaur became a human.

What the creator writes into the DNA of the master will only reproduce and transmit those same species characteristics and will do it immediately, not after 100 million copies have been produced.

All DNA that was written by our creator has always and will always reproduce only after its own kind. He locked the DNA into the genetic code and has no intention of giving the key to you or me, can you imagine if He did?

You may have been told that you are a silly old cow, or have been accused of acting the goat and may have been a rude pig from time to time, but that is as far as the similarity goes, you are a human and so you will only ever reproduce humans.

I have stayed on this point to show you that you were born on purpose, for a purpose and to dispel the lie that you just sort of came into being by some accident. The reason that millions of people feel hopeless, without a vision or a future, is because they have bought that blatant lie.

What sort of hope and a future or self-image would you expect to have if you originated from a green piece of slime?

I have set aside an entire chapter about the evolution theory or the monkey business and have included statements, quotes and admissions by the most renowned evolutionists, professors, doctors, biologists and other science experts of all time.

You will be amazed what they have said about their inability to show any evidence of the theory of evolution and on that note the word theory means among other things an "idea" or a "notion". Do anything you want to do, but do not put your entire life and future in the hands of an idea or a notion, you are far too valuable for that.

- Back to the facts, when cells divide DNA takes the form of chromosomes which are the units carrying the genes that pass hereditary features from parents to offspring.

- Once again human body cells normally contain 46 distinctive chromosomes, however a sperm and an egg contain 23 each. When these two marry or unite they bring their 23 chromosomes together, making one completely new cell which is you and you the human embryo now have 46 chromosomes that carry a unique never to be repeated combination of genes.

- The human embryo is not just simply a set of instructions for making a new human being, like a plan is to build a house.

- A plan is inert and cannot carry out instructions, but the embryo is active and begins work on itself at once, what a miracle!

- A house needs carpenters, electricians, bricklayers and plumbers to complete it; but the embryo has the ability to grow spontaneously. It moves on to other phases of development, constructing the skeleton, flesh, nerve connections, waste disposal system, air conditioning and so on of the human body.

- After a house is built a plan remains separate; but the embryo is already an essential human by virtue of its genes and is the blueprint or master copy, builder and "house" all together.

OUR INCREDIBLE BODY

- Doubling a child's height on their second birthday gives a close estimate of their final adult height. A boy of two is 49.5 per cent of his adult height; a girl of two is 52.8 per cent of her adult height.

- Each finger and toenail takes about 6 months to grow from its base to the tip.

- During pregnancy a woman's blood volume can increase by up to 50 per cent to a total of 6.75 litres (12 pints) as a reserve against possible loss of blood during delivery.

- The brain accounts for about 3 per cent of our body weight, but it uses 20 per cent of all the oxygen we breathe, 20 per cent of the calories in the food we eat and about 15 per cent of our body's blood supply.

- The adult human body contains approximately 650 muscles, over 100 joints, 100,000 km (60,000 miles) of blood vessels and 13,000 nerve cells.

- An adult has 206 bones—nearly half of them in the hands and feet. A baby has 300 bones at birth, but 94 of them fuse together during childhood.

- Human bone is as strong as granite in supporting weight. A block the size of a matchbox can support 9 tonnes (8.86 tonnes) - four times as much as concrete.

- A man's testicles manufacture 10 million new sperm cells a day—enough in six months to populate the entire world.

- The heart beats more than 2,000 million times during the average human life span and in that time will pump around 500 million litres (110 million gallons) of blood. Even during sleep, the fist-sized heart of an adult pumps about 340 litres (75 gallons) an hour—enough to fill an average car's petrol tank every 7 minutes. It generates enough muscle power every day to lift an average-sized car about 15m (50ft).

- The average pulse rate is 70-72 beats per minute at rest for adult males and 78-82 beats per minute for adult females. The rate can increase to as much as 200 beats per minute during violent exercise.

YOU CAN'T ARGUE WITH THE FACTS

- The lungs contain a total of 300,000 million capillaries which are tiny blood vessels and which would stretch 2,400km (1,500 miles) if laid end to end.

- The body of an average adult contains 45 litres (79 pints) of water, about 65 per cent of their weight.

- The stomach's digestive acids are strong enough to dissolve zinc. But the cells in the stomach lining are renewed so quickly—500,000 cells are replaced every minute and the entire lining every three days so that the acids do not have time to dissolve the lining.

- The total number of genes required to create the entire human population that lives on the face of the earth today could fit into a thimble.

- By the time you turn seventy, your heart has beat some two billion five hundred thousand times based on an average of 70 beats per minute.

Let us examine the difference between a million and a billion for just a moment. If I had one million dollars, I could give you $1,000 every day for three years before I ran out of money, however if I had one billion dollars I could give you $1,000 every day for three thousand years before I ran out of money. Therefore if I had two billion five hundred thousand dollars I could give you $1,000 every day for seven thousand five hundred years before I was broke. What an incredible machine we have inside us, maybe we should patent it, oh sorry we are too late God already has.

- If you were to tie all of your capillaries and veins together they would reach 96,500 kilometres. Using the imagination for a moment, let us say that we exposed one of the capillaries in your arm and tied it to the back of an aircraft, so as the aircraft flew your capillaries and veins would unwind like a ball of string. If the aircraft was to travel at 1,000 kilometres per hour, it would have to fly for just over 4 days and travel more than twice around the entire earth before your veins and capillaries would completely unwind, by the way the distance around the earth at 23º North is 40,074 kilometres.

- Each kidney contains some 1 million individual filters and between them the two kidneys filter an average of 1.3 litres (2.2 pints) of blood in a minute. The waste products are expelled as urine at the rate of about 1.4 litres (2.5 pints) a day.

- The body's entire blood supply—some, 4.5 litres (8 pints) washes through the lungs about once a minute. Human red blood corpuscles are created by bone marrow at the rate of about 1.2 million corpuscles per second. Each lives for 100-120 days. In a lifetime the marrow creates about half a tonne (1,102lbs) of red corpuscles.

- The body's largest organ is the skin. In an adult man it covers about $1.9m^2$ (20 square feet); a woman has about $1.6m^2$ (17 square feet). The skin is constantly flaking away and being completely replaced by new tissue about once every 50 days. On average, each person sheds about 18kg (40 lb) of skin during his or her lifetime.

- The smallest human muscle is in the ear; it is a little over 1mm (.04 in) long. The ear also contains one of the few parts of the body which has no blood vessels. Cells in part of the inner ear, where sound vibrations are converted to nerve impulses, are fed by a constant bath of fluid instead of blood—otherwise the sensitive nerves would be deafened by the sound of the body's own pulse.

- You grow by about 8mm (0.31 in) every night when you are asleep, but shrink to your former height the following day. During the day, the cartilage discs in the spine are squeezed like sponges by gravity while you stand or sit. But at night, when you lie down to sleep, the pressure is relieved and the discs swell again. For the same reason, astronauts can be temporarily 50mm (2 in) taller after a long spaceflight.

- Besides water, the body contains an assortment of other substances. On average, it has enough lime to whitewash a small shed, the equivalent in carbon of a 12.7kg (28 lb) bag of coke, enough phosphorus to make 2,200 match heads, about a spoonful of sulphur, enough iron to make a 25mm (1 in) nail — and about 30g (1 oz) of other metals <u>and all can be found in the dust of the ground</u>.

- The focusing muscles of the eye move about 100,000 times a day. To give the leg muscles the equivalent amount of exercise would involve walking 80km (50 miles) a day.

- The retina inside the eye covers about 650mm^2 (1 sq in) and contains 137 million light—sensitive cells: 130 million rod cells for black and white vision and 7 million cone cells for colour vision.

- The average person in the West eats 50 tonnes (49.2 tonnes) of food and drinks 50,000 litres (11,000 gallons) of liquid during their lifetime.

- Each square inch of your skin consists of twenty feet of blood vessels and 45 miles or around 70 kilometres of nerves in the skin. The next time you go for a drive put on your trip meter and measure it, you will be amazed.

- We should remember and practice this all the time, it takes 17 muscles to smile and 43 to frown; smiling is much better.

- Laughing lowers levels of stress hormones and strengthens the immune system. Six year olds laugh an average of 300 times a day. Adults only laugh 15 to 100 times a day.

- The largest cell in the human body is the female ovum or egg cell. It is about 1/180 inch in diameter. The smallest cell in the body is the male sperm cell. It takes about 175,000 sperm cells to weigh as much as a single egg cell.

- Three hundred million human cells die every minute in our body.

- You not only have unique fingerprints and DNA, but you also have a unique tongue print.

Not one of your body functions we are about to examine could have developed from a stage that was more primitive, all must have been functioning, as they are now to exist at all. The investigation of the structure and the complexity of your body can only bring one conclusion and that is, the great Giver of Life is a Master Craftsman beyond compare and beyond our ordinary understanding.

For a moment let us examine the cell for it is the essential element in the "make-up" of all life. The cell we are about to look at is the body cell or the Somatic Cell. This cell is invisible to the naked eye and yet this minute speck has proved to be, biologically, a living, working, compartmented, organised, and extremely complex chemical factory. This has all been revealed to us today under the tremendous magnification of the electron microscope.

Chemically it has in its composition carbon, hydrogen, oxygen, nitrogen, sulphur, phosphorus, chlorine, potassium, iron, fluorine, and iodine. Within the cell are organisms called enzymes, one of the most complicated, mysterious, and marvellous things known to man. These enzymes in conjunction with the numerous, exceedingly involved molecules, can do what no chemical laboratory made by man could ever do and do it quickly, efficiently and continuously.

There are many compartments in this living factory, involving millions of active sub-cells, all working to a pre-determined code (set of instructions written into the DNA) and within the nucleus of the cell, are the chromosomes.

The cell of every living thing has its fixed number of chromosomes, which form a combination lock. This locks up the species and compels them to obey the universal law that every living thing will reproduce after its own kind.

> "[11] *Then God said, "Let the land produce vegetation: seed-bearing plants and trees on the land that bear fruit with seed in it, according to their various kinds." And it was so.* [12] *The land produced vegetation: plants bearing seed according to their kinds and trees bearing fruit with seed in it according to their kinds. And God saw that it was good.* [13] *And there was evening, and there was morning—the third day.* [24] *And God said, "Let the land produce liv-*

ing creatures according to their kinds: livestock, creatures that move along the ground, and wild animals, each according to its kind." And it was so. [25]*God made the wild animals according to their kinds, the livestock according to their kinds, and all the creatures that move along the ground according to their kinds. And God saw that it was good."*
Genesis 1:11-13, 24 -25

This is vitally important because within the chromosomes are the infinitely minute and wonderful genes, several million of them, which like the notes on a piano, provide for an almost endless variety within the species and I repeat within the species!

One of the most marvellous facts about the cell is that it cannot grow or develop gradually and only a living cell can produce a cell because to live it must be a complete living unit.

How then does it multiply?

This is one of the most wonderful and mysterious things ever witnessed by man.

In a process called "mitosis" the cell divides and amid intense activity, both visible and invisible, the cell becomes two living factories and each again does the same to become, (1) (2) (4) (8) (16) (32) (64) (128) (256) (512) (1024) (2048) (4096) (8192) (16,384) (32,768) (65,536) (131,072) (262,144) (524,288) (1,048,576) (2,097,152) (4,194,304) (8,388,608) (16,777,216) and so on.

Each body demands different forms of cells and the implanted plan in the cell knows exactly what combinations of chemicals from the storehouse to call upon and which departments to call into service to provide and produce the particular cells required for the part of the body being built at the time, just like the duplication process of the movie master of The Ten Commandments. I am writing this chapter on my laptop computer locked away in a room in a beautiful and peaceful environment on the Northern Beaches of Sydney, Australia and each time I write 50 or so words I save them to the hard disk and also to a floppy disk just in case my computer crashes and I lose what I have written. What I have saved is exactly what I have written and in a million years time it will remain the same, just like what our Creator wrote into the human DNA is the same today, tomorrow, and forever more.

He wrote it, He saved it and He alone has access to the combination, but He has given us the awesome joy and responsibility to play a significant role in the creation process and the nurturing of His children.

Because we are created in God's image He considers us to be the highest expression of His creative genius.

CHAPTER TWO
YOU CAN'T HAVE CREATION WITHOUT A CREATOR

The following is just a glimpse of what you will read in the chapter about evolution but because it is very important to what we are discussing right now I have inserted this quote here.

NOTHING CANNOT PRODUCE MATTER

Meldau goes on to say, "Nothing cannot produce matter, (Atoms) Genesis 1:1 and Hebrews 11:3 give the only answer. Between matter and motion there is a similar gulf. There is no greater attested fact of science, than the fact that it takes power to put inert matter into motion. No evolutionary theory we have ever heard of attempts to explain the origin of both matter and motion unless it concedes a prime cause— God. Life cannot come into being except it comes from previous life."

It is a universal and inarguable scientific fact that to have creation you must have a creator. You cannot have a motor vehicle unless someone created it, a hamburger, a lounge suite, a guitar or anything else.

That being the case then you could not be created without a creator because it would defy scientific facts and universal laws. Things are created on purpose and for a purpose, but you are not a thing, you are the most incredible creation of all. The aircraft and the motor vehicle and everything else made by the hand of man had its origin in the dust of the ground. If you have a challenge with believing that anything can be created without a creator, then just sit there for an hour and try to work it out in your head.

You will not be able to because it is a universal law that does not bow down to our finite thinking.

Did you ever try to imagine nothing when you were a child? I would lie awake at night and try to picture nothing, actually removing everything until there was only blackness or whiteness or transparentness left.

All of these remaining images are something, blackness is something an empty space is something and nothing is something. I gave up after many times of trying to imagine nothing and the same outcome will occur when you try to prove that something can be created without a creator.

The Bible says the following about your creation when God was speaking by His Holy Spirit prophetically through King David.

> "*¹³For you created my inmost being; you knit me together in my mother's womb. ¹⁴I praise you because I am fearfully and wonderfully made; your works are wonderful, I know that full well. ¹⁵My frame was not hidden from you when I was made in the secret place. When I was woven together in the depths of the earth, ¹⁶Your eyes saw my unformed body. All the days ordained for me were written in your book before one of them came to be.*"
> Psalms 139:13-16

If we have established that you can't have creation without a creator, then the Bible is right because God would be the only one with the creative ability to design you and me, or perhaps you and I could do it, couldn't we?

If He did create you and me and did so in His own image, can you imagine Him doing so without a plan or purpose and not only that, but to bury in the ground at our time of death the very image of Himself to a lost eternity?

> "*²⁶Then God said, 'Let us make man in our image, in our likeness, and let them rule over the fish of the sea and the birds of the air, over the livestock, over all the earth, and over all the creatures that move along the ground.' ²⁷So God created man in his own image, in the image of God he created him; male and female he created them.*"
> Genesis 1:26-27

Would you bury in the ground for all eternity with no further value, hope or use, your highest expression of creative genius that you actually created in your own image and if you wouldn't then why would God?

YOU CAN'T HAVE CREATION WITHOUT A CREATOR

The Bible says that He created us in His image and so I wonder what would lead Him to bury the very image of Himself to a lost eternity, with no future and no hope. If you would bury your highest expression of creative genius, then maybe you already have and so you must finish reading this book because it will show you how to resurrect all that you have buried including yourself.

God did allow Himself to be buried once and it was not to a lost eternity, but was all part of His incredible plan and purpose as you will read later, don't turn there now just wait till you get there.

The Jumbo Jet, the Motor Vehicle, the White House, Yankee Stadium, the Golden Gate Bridge, the Titanic, the Apollo Space Ships, the Teaspoon, the Watch, the Locomotive and the like, were all created for a specific purpose and they all came from the dust of the ground. Every single part of them had their origin in the earth—please remember this as you read on.

I find it staggering to contemplate that all of these items were created for a specific purpose and yet many believe that the human being, the most incredible and miraculous creation of all somehow evolved and just sort of happened due to a whole lot of chemical and biological reactions without a creator or purpose, or without a plan of any kind, you are kidding!

If you had the ability to make a human being would you do so without a reason?

I was just thinking this morning about how precious money is to people, even though after all it is just a piece of paper, but we never see anyone destroying it or throwing it into the trash. Money was created on purpose, for a specific purpose and it is a great thing unless we have the wrong personality behind it.

If you gave money to Mother Theresa she would have done incredible things with it, like feed the hungry, help the poor and the lost, however if you gave that same money to someone with evil intent then the potential for good changes to a potential for evil.

You often hear the old saying that "money is the root of all evil." That is not correct as that term actually comes from the Bible and it reads as follows.

> "*9People who want to get rich fall into temptation and a trap and into many foolish and harmful desires that plunge men into ruin and destruction. 10For the love of money is a root of all kinds of evil. Some people, eager for money, have wandered from the faith and pierced themselves with many griefs."*
> I Timothy 6:9-10

God created us in His image and yet He has given us a free will to decide whether we will be like the money living our lives for good or for evil.

The main point I wanted to make in this chapter was to establish that you cannot have creation without a creator, and now that we have laid that important foundation we can start our incredible journey through the unseen world.

CHAPTER THREE
THEY'RE OFF AND RACING

When sperm cells are about to be sent forth they become very alert and fidgety, just like the competitors at the beginning of an iron man race. The incredible thing is that they know their race is about to begin, because this instinct was written into their genetic code when they were created.

Let's imagine for a moment that we are back at the time of your conception and this race that you are about to embark on has 80 million and 800 million starters.

Out of these millions and millions of starters there will not only be one winner, but there will only be one survivor, (except in the case of multiple births) and that is YOU!

In a normal swimming or running race even though there is only

THEY'RE OFF AND RACING

one winner the other competitors do not die as a result of participating, however the other competitors in your race all died except you and the key point to remember here is <u>that someone had to die, that you could live</u>.

Dead sperm release a chemical, which breaks down the tough outer coating of the egg so that conception can actually take place and therefore if sperm do not die, then you could not live.

This race is incredibly difficult and physically demanding for even the fittest of the competitors and this sacrifice of life has been at the forefront of human existence from the very beginning. Millions of people have given their lives in order to protect their loved ones or their country and we will talk later about the ultimate sacrifice that was made so that you may live not just in this life, but in the life to come.

The distance that you had to travel inside the reproductive tract was only 7 to 15 inches or so, but you were not even visible to the human eye and so you travelled many miles or kilometres, as we will discover.

If you had to swim for 12 hours at the normal sperm speed rate of around 3.8 kilometres per hour you would have travelled the equivalent of 46 kms or around 32 miles. If it took 24 hours you would travel the equivalent of 93 kilometres or 60 miles and if it took the full 36 hours you would have travelled the equivalent of an incredible 140 kilometres or 93 miles.

These distances and calculations may vary but please focus on the point here and not the mathematics. If you had to swim for 36 hours to reach your other half, the egg cell and you lost your way by swimming around in circles most of the time you would have travelled the equivalent of around 140 kilometres.

That makes you better than most of the world's greatest marathon swimmers and they always swim on flat surfaces, you were often swimming directly towards the sky because your mother would have spent much of this 12 to 36 hour period standing upright and therefore you were swimming vertically.

Just imagine for a moment that you are swimming in a race that is often directly up stream for 12 to 36 hours without a road map and unable to see even one inch in front of you. You were then told that you are racing against 80 million to 800 million fierce competitors who are all bent on killing you so that they could claim the winner's prize.

Well you can stop imagining because you did swim in that race and not only that, but you were declared the winner.

Have you ever seen a triathlon race with the fighting for position that happens when only 100 to 200 swimmers enter the water together. Well multiply that out to as many as 800,000,000 competitors trying to kill each other, but the great news is that try as they may, they could not get you because you were the chosen one.

MATHEMATICAL CALCULATIONS

The sperm cell seems a little bit awkward from the result of my research. It is still controversial as regard to the accurate figures in academic research done on the speed of sperm cells. So I chose the standard speed used in one scale up analysis with Salmons and Sperm Wales, which is 35μm/s (micrometer per second).

However, "The speed of a sperm cell is never constant and is affected mostly by its physiology and environment and also due to a sperm cell's tiny size (25 μm) and the fluid—filled environment; the viscosity of the sperm cell's surroundings produces the greatest effect on its swimming speed rather than inertial forces that larger organisms would encounter. The size of the sperm cell I use here is 55μm among different sources. It seems that 7 inches once it arrives in the reproductive tract is the standard size of the distance to the ovum, which I also take into our calculation and so here is the result. This does not include the distance travelled to reach the reproductive tract, which could easily double this distance.

1. How long does it take a sperm cell to get to the ovum? 7 inch x 25.4mm/inch x 1000μm/mm/35μm/s/3600s/ hour =1.41hr. Though humans walk straight a comparable test can still be done. Here I use 170cm as an average height of human beings. Here is the scaled up speed as a human being. V/170cm = 35μm/s/55μm so v = 108.18cm/s=1.08m/s = 3.894km/h

2. How far can you travel at the scaled up speed as a sperm cell get to the human ovum?

3. 3.894km/h x 1.41h = 5.5km

INFORMATION ADDED

The calculations are based on the sperm cell swimming straight to the ovum (egg). It can take up to 36 hours for sperm to reach the egg and therefore if it took 36 hours the distance travelled could be around 140 km or 90 miles.

Not long ago I saw a satellite photo taken from outer space of the largest crowd ever gathered in one place. It was a crowd in India that were washing away their sins in the Ganges River. Let me assure you that your sins can be washed away but not in the Ganges River as you will read later. You could clearly see the satellite photo of this crowd of 30 million from outer space, now multiply it by 20 or so and that will give you some idea of what you were up against.

Recent research in the medical science world suggests that many sperm during the race turn around, attack and kill other sperm.

This leaves a clear pathway for the others to travel and just maybe this is part of their job, to make the way clear for the chosen one which was you.

It is an awesome thought and whether it is correct or not does not change the fact, that there are no ifs and no buts, you won the race and that is the end of it.

Maybe the other sperm in your race were just there to encourage and put pressure on you to go for it all the way to the finish line, just like the pacemaker does for the athletes in big races like the world championships and then they were commissioned by God to die so that you might live. (someone else died for you so why not them?)

By the end of the race there are normally only a few thousand competitors left and these also must die before the finish line to create the necessary environment for you to unite with your other half, the egg and for conception to take place. As we said before it is the death of these sperm that softens the hard shell on the egg to allow the sperm to penetrate.

THEY'RE OFF AND RACING

I can imagine the other competitors standing on the side of the race track encouraging you to keep going and telling you when you got tired, that you are the chosen but you must keep running all the way to the finish line.

Well the human race is just like that, it is a race that must be run and there is something amazing that happens to us on the inside when we have to struggle and fight for something in order to win.

The most precious stone known to man is the diamond, but for a diamond to have great value it must undergo and overcome the enormous pressure that is applied while it is being created in the deepest parts of the earth.

If a diamond can stand up to the pressure of the earth that crushes around it and is then born without flaw, it will be considered amongst the most precious and valuable of all diamonds and yet it is no more than a piece of rock, that like everything else was created in the depths of the earth. Man places incredible value on this piece of rock and on many occasions has killed people for it.

The diamond maker receives it when it looks like any other worthless piece of rock, but he can see the great potential that it has long before he actually begins to carefully and skillfully sculpt it. Once his masterpiece of fine jewellery is complete, it can on many occasions have a price tag that is in the millions of dollars.

The diamond is considered amongst the most valuable of all worldly treasures, but you are priceless and also stood up under the immense pressure that was applied to you while you were being created and born.

Your value cannot be measured by the world's standards, because

THE KEY TO LIFE

The Creator of diamonds and everything else that has ever been, created you.

In order to try and get a piece of this rock which is valued in carats, people have not only been killed but have been prepared to risk their lives for it.

Your value cannot be measured and someone didn't just risk their life but actually gave their life and was murdered in order that you may have life.

This was not dependant on whether you were without flaw or not, as this diamond maker could see a potential and value in you that others could not.

Just as others had to die in the womb that you might have this life, this diamond maker died that you might have eternal life.

If you want to give birth to something in your life whether it is a vision, a child, a career, an invention or something else there will be a time of conception, a time of pregnancy, a time of labour, a time of being stretched and of experiencing the contractions that come with the beginning of the birthing process and then the pain of actually giving birth.

Many of you reading this right now would not have been told what a great joy it was to watch you being born, or what a great joy it was to give birth to you. As I write this I can sense the pain you are feeling at this very moment, but there is good news because you to can experience the joy of giving birth to something and just like an ecstatic mother you will then see that the pain of giving birth will pale to insignificance compared to the joy and pleasure of giving birth to your own vision, child, career or destiny.

THEY'RE OFF AND RACING

We can give birth to negative outcomes in life, just as easily as we give birth to positive outcomes as it all depends where we are focused. Being negative can have power over being positive, because being negative requires no forward momentum or action but being positive does. If you want to be negative you can just sit there and pull everything and everyone down around you, including yourself.

Negative people operate under the law of detraction and repel everyone and everything around them, but we can stop this law operating in our lives by changing our way of thinking and placing a door at the entry of our heart and our mind, that only has one key. That door remains locked until you want to open it and this should be only to let in positive people, thoughts and actions. We have no choice but to reap what we sow into our minds so do not give out keys or leave the door open, because you may find unwanted guests living in your heart and mind.

If we sow positive thoughts and actions into our hearts and minds we will reap a harvest of positive outcomes, but just remember the same law applies if we sow negative thoughts and actions. Make sure that there is no back door to your heart and mind, because negative and wrong thoughts always try and enter through the back door when you least expect them.

The sower of these wrong and negative thoughts then has the audacity to come around the front, look you in the eye and accuse you of having them.

These accusations are always the forerunner to depression, negativity, self-doubt, fear and poor self-image.

As a sperm cell if you had decided not to run the race you would not be here today. You won that race because written into your genetic code was the spirit of a winner and so there is no argument, you are here because you won a race and you have been set up for success. You can never say that you have never won anything and have never been successful.

If you choose to be positive and achieve something in your life your first decision right now must be to put action into your vision, your dreams, your goals and your desires and you will see how to do this later.

Let me say this, you will pay a price for failure and you will also pay a price for success, so which price would you prefer to pay?

Fear is to believe in what you can't see and faith is to believe in what you can't see, so where would you prefer to live?

You really have no other choice, as you do not know what will happen tomorrow, no matter how much you worry about it. Fear will bring the worst upon you because you will always reap what you sow, but faith will bring the best upon you for that very same reason. We see wars and threatening of wars all over the world today, but the biggest and longest lasting wars are fought in the minds of men, women and children.

All physical wars that have been or are being fought have started as a seed in the minds of human beings and whether they were motivated by an offence, a religious disagreement or just plain greed, that is how they all started and then they happened in the physical world.

THEY'RE OFF AND RACING

TIMING IS OF THE ESSENCE

From the time your father was about fifteen years of age he produced around 10 million sperm cells every day and that would be sufficient to populate the entire earth in six months. I am not going to do the mathematical calculation here but just imagine for a moment how many sperm cells your father would have produced in one year at 10,000,000 per day and if you were conceived when your father was 25 years of age, he would have produced enough sperm cells to have populated the entire earth 20 times.

If there were three children born in your family only three of those trillions and trillions of sperm cells actually ever won the race to be born and you were one of them, WOW, you are a winner aren't you!

You could have been created as a sperm cell at any other time during those ten years and had never been born at all, but the fact is that you were not.

You were created at exactly the right moment, of exactly the right hour, of exactly the right day, of exactly the right week, of exactly the right month, of exactly the right year, of exactly the right decade, of exactly the right century and if you were not then you would not be here, do you get it yet!

Your mother and father not only had to meet at a particular time in history, but they actually had to meet in the first place because if they didn't you could not be created. I know right now some of you may wish that they never did meet because of the tragic circumstances of your birth. I also realise that if you were the result of a sperm donor or the like, then your mother and father probably never did meet, so please read my heart here because it changes nothing about your awesome future and destiny.

Put the book down for a moment and imagine the task in front of you if you were the creator of all things and that you intended to create every person on purpose, for a purpose and to be born at a certain time in history.

This would mean that from the very beginning you would have to plan and co-ordinate the perfect time of the creation, maturity and release of every sperm and egg that was ever made in order that you could be here.

You might be thinking that it all happened by chance, probably the same chance that this book explodes in your hands right now, is blown into 250,000,000 pieces and as each piece lands on the floor it comes back together as the book that is in your hands right now. I do not have enough faith to believe in chance and in fact if it is all based on chance then faith is useless.

You are here, you won, and if you didn't then someone else would be here in your place and they are not, you are and you are an incredible miracle and were born a winner; so keep on winning and go for it.

The race that you embarked on in your mother's womb was a race against time and if you did not arrive at your destination within 36 hours your chance at life was gone forever. Not only that but if you lost your way, got trampled in the rush, failed to finish, died or got pipped at the post you would not have been born.

As we established before but need to clarify again, medical science tells us that when the race is about to begin the competitors become very excited and their tales start to thrash from side to side almost like

THEY'RE OFF AND RACING

a formula one racing car would sit at the starting line and rev its engine in anticipation of the flag falling and the race beginning. It is important to remember here that all sperm are not the same as DNA has proven that they are all uniquely different.

You had to swim up stream and through a dark tunnel, which was the reproductive tract of your mother. This can be likened to a maze where you had to swim against a torrential river full of debris and obstacles and the resistance and pressure you had to face would have been incredible.

Resistance is very important because it builds stamina, determination and endurance and when you have overcome the resistance you become stronger than you ever were before.

In the womb you needed to face this kind of resistance and overcome it so that you could finish and win the race to be born. It also laid a foundation of determination, patience and endurance for the further 9 months you would need to spend in your mother's womb facing many other life threatening challenges before you were ready to face the incredible pressure and risk of actually being born.

Resistance is an awesome force and should be one of your closest friends because it will build you into a strong and determined person.

You must resist, resisting the resistance and except the fact that it is a creative force designed to build into you the spirit of a winner.

Initially resistance may slow you down and may even break you down but if you have unwavering determination, purpose, faith and vision by seeing your goal before you achieve it, resistance will become your best friend.

Body builders must face resistance every time they train if they want to increase the size of their muscles and so they lift weights which build their muscles. To increase strength and build endurance they have to overcome the resistance with utter determination so they will achieve their goal of building bigger muscles.

Their muscles do not return to their original size after they have finished each session but are broken down and actually bleed because of the pressure of trying to lift these heavy weights. The brain tells the muscles to build bigger and stronger so that they can lift the weights that the body builder is forcing them to lift.

If the muscles do not grow, it means the body builder is training in his comfort zone and in my experience of life, nothing of any significance happens in your comfort zone.

As soon as the body builder stops lifting heavier and heavier weights or stops the resistance by way of doing repetitions his muscles will stop growing, so you must treat resistance as your friend just as the body builders do. They also do repetition after repetition, because repetition is the key to building muscles and repetition is the key to learning. Let the resistance that comes against you in life build you into a stronger person and as they may break you down from time to time, keep building yourself up, not with pride but with utter determination to break through in all your endeavours.

Applying heat to gold in its raw state produces pure gold and this heat causes the scum to come to the surface so it can be scooped away. The heat is then turned up a little until more scum comes to the surface and this process continues until finally there is pure gold.

This same process can occur in your life when the heat is on, so don't avoid the heat but welcome it and let the rubbish in your life come to the surface, deal with it and then go forward.

Eventually you will become like pure gold and be able to stand up under the heat and the pressure that comes against you every day of your life.

There is not a person on the face of the planet who has not had to deal with the heat and the pressure that causes rubbish in their life to surface. If you deal with it right then and there you will be able to move on, but do not beat yourself up because overcoming the rubbish does not happen in one day, but it does happen daily.

PART TWO – LIVE A WINNER

CHAPTER FOUR
THE LONG ARM OF THE LAW

Rear Admiral D.V. Gallery, U.S.N. Saturday evening post wrote, "the stars in their orbits and velocities through the heavens faithfully obey a great code of law. Earth's scientists can quote and explain this code in great detail, until you ask. Whence came these laws"?

When we look at the marvels of this universe we can only but agree with the writer who said. "It were as easy to believe that Milton's Paradise were set up in all it's stately march of balanced syllables by an ape, or that the letters of balanced syllables by an ape, or that the letters composing it had been blown together by a whirlwind, as to believe that the visible universe about us, built upon mathematical laws, knitted together by a million correspondences, and crowned thick with marks of purpose, is the work of a mindless force." Dr Fitchett.

The evidence that you and I were created is all around us and can be seen in abundance by all who will stop and think.

SCIENCE TELLS US

- In chemistry, no two substances can unite without observing definite mathematical laws.

- In music all whole tones are multiples of eleven.

- What about the awesome timetable of the Universe, the incredible speed of the planets, all travelling on their appointed course like a huge railway system and yet none colliding. So accurate is their timetable that their relative positions can be set down to a future date.

- The surface speed of the earth is approximately 1,100 miles an hour and if it dropped to say 110 we would be roasted in a 240 hour day and any life that survived would be frozen in a similarly long night.

- The earth is tilted at 23 degrees and if it wasn't we would have no seasons.

- If the crust of the earth was but a few feet thicker there would be no oxygen and hence no life could exist.

- If the sun was much closer we would roast and if it was further away we would freeze.

- If the moon was any nearer the tides would sweep over everything except the mountains.
- If the air had been much thinner, many disasters would overwhelm us and yet the fact is that we find thousands of laws combining to make life on earth possible.

When the heavens and the earth were created, they were so within the boundaries of universal laws and these laws were designed to keep order.

While we operate within the boundaries of these laws we will not suffer the consequences of being a lawbreaker.

There is something in the heart of mankind that likes to stretch the boundaries as far as we can and this often results in us breaking these laws and then having to suffer the relative consequences.

These laws remain constant and whether we are rich or poor, the leader of a powerful nation or we spend our days sitting on a park bench these laws will not bow down to us.

Here are just four of the thousands of laws.

- The Law of Gravity
- The Law of Reproduction
- The Law of Sowing and Reaping
- The Law of Aerodynamics

THE LONG ARM OF THE LAW

THE LAW OF GRAVITY

If you climb up on a 60 metre high building and jump off without a parachute or other apparatus that works to overcome the law of gravity you will hit the ground and from that height, most probably die.

The reason that this will happen to you is because very simply, you broke the law. "What law did I break? There is no law that says I can't jump off a building if I choose to."

That may be true however you did break the law of gravity and you will suffer the consequences.

We can deny and fight against these laws as much as we like, but they continue to operate the way they want to despite our opinions and they have the authority to do just that.

Imagine if these laws were not constant and there was no order to them, so that one morning you wake up, get out of bed and just float away into space.

The law of gravity keeps us earth bound while we are in the earth's atmosphere, however when we move outside the earth's atmosphere the law of gravity does not have the same authority over us.

If we live within the boundaries of this law, we need not suffer the consequences of the lawbreakers. The same applies if we obey the laws of the land; as they are in place to give us boundaries of protection and accountability. Many have said if it feels good then do it and although that may sound great many of those people have died in horrific circumstances long before they should have. Boundaries are a good thing because they keep us safe and all champions in any field of endeavour operate within them.

Let me share a story with you about a game of Rugby which is played in a particular maximum-security prison. This game is called CRASH and the reason that they call it that is because there are no rules, no boundaries and no penalties, just simply the last man standing.

Many of the men who play this game will spend the rest of their lives in prison and so they play the game as a form of release. Visitors to the prison are allowed to watch the prisoners play and at one time a group of people were granted permission to interview the prisoners and the spectators in order to find out what they thought about the game. Not one of the prisoners or one of the spectators actually enjoyed the game and the common reasons were that the game required no skill as there were no boundaries. The game of Rugby as it is played around the world is played in boundary lines and with very specific rules and regulations.

These rules and regulations are in place for many reasons including safety for the players and enjoyment for the spectators. The players are free to display their skill within the boundaries of the rugby laws, which are designed to keep them responsible, accountable and safe. If you abide by the rules you will be protected by the referee, however if you don't you will be cautioned or penalised, sent off or even rubbed out by the tribunal. Not because they are picking on you but because you did not obey the laws of the game as they are set out.

Whether in business, sport, acting or any other field of endeavour champions enjoy success because they operate within specific laws and boundaries.

THE LONG ARM OF THE LAW

Many of the prisoners who play this game are serving life sentences because they did not operate within the boundaries of the law of the land.

This is devastating for the prisoners and also in many cases for the innocent victims that had to suffer the consequences of what someone else sowed.

It has been said that more than 90% of prisoners both male and female have suffered some form of abuse in their lives especially when they were children. This abuse creates poor self image, anger, desire for revenge, bitterness, hopelessness and feelings of betrayal.

The words of death and the physical abuse that many of these people have had to suffer reproduced itself in them and often the very abuse they had to suffer they inflicted on others.

Millions of innocent people have had to suffer devastation inflicted by others which just shows what a broken and lost world we are living in.

Whether you have been abused or you have abused others I am going to show you as you read on how you can be completely set free, just as I was!

THE LAW OF REPRODUCTION

DNA gives permission for cells to reproduce and transmit <u>same species</u> characteristics from one generation to another.

The law or the rules of the game of life which are locked into DNA is interwoven with the law of reproduction and throughout this book you will see this linking together. Everything in the entire universe was designed by the same architect and has His fingerprint and His signature on all His universal laws and His creation.

If two elephants mate they will very rarely give birth to a buffalo and in fact they never do, that would be ridiculous because we can only ever reproduce after our own kind.

When a male and a female human being join together in sexual union and the woman becomes pregnant, she will give birth to a human being.

Can you imagine if there was no order or laws in place and you went to hospital to see your new baby, only to find that it was half human and half antelope. Don't laugh too hard because this is the sort of garbage that the theory of evolution has been trying to sell for centuries.

The law of reproduction operates not only in the physical world, but also in the spiritual or unseen world and just because we cannot see something does not mean it is not there, it just means that our eyes are unable to see into that realm. We cannot see the wind but we can feel it and so we believe it is there, just as we cannot see radio waves but we can hear the result of them so we know they are there.

We cannot see God either but he has displayed his creation everywhere which includes the radio waves and the wind so why do so many think that He is a figment of the imagination?

I have met many people over the years that do not believe in God and have said that they are atheists and you may have said the very same thing, so let me share a story with you. I have a friend who was the Assistant Superintendent of the Police Traffic Department and over a long period of time attended 53 particular motor vehicle accidents that either resulted in a death after he had arrived at the scene, or that had died later in hospital. He noticed something quite amazing as all but one of these 53 people were either screaming out to God for help or they were cursing God. He decided to do some research into their backgrounds and his investigations revealed something just as amazing, of these 53 people that died only one of them professed to know God or classified themselves as a Christian.

It is very hard to find an atheist in the middle of a fire, an earthquake, a hurricane, when your plane is about to crash, in a car accident or when you are facing certain death.

So why is our natural response in these situations to scream out to God?

The Bible says that God created man in His image and therefore His DNA is in our heart, but just like any other relationship He also gave us a free will to choose to accept Him or not. The Bible says;

> "*[11]He has made everything beautiful in its time.*
> *He has also set eternity in the hearts of men; yet they cannot fathom what God has done from beginning to end.*"
> Ecclesiastes 3:11

If you give someone a free will, it does not give you a license to take that away from him or her if and when you feel like it, even if you are God.

God will not break His own laws and when he says He gave you a free will He means a free will all the time.

Imagine for a moment giving your children the free will to do what ever they chose to do even if you knew that a wrong decision by them could result in their death, well that is the choice that God has given you.

Leaders who lack people skills and cannot retain staff normally find the only people that will stay with them are those who operate and behave very much like they do. Because of the law of reproduction they have reproduced after their own kind.

People who suffer from poor self-image often have children that suffer the same problem because they have lived with it for many years, they have inherited it from their parents. Not genetically but by living in that environment for so long they have inherited the spiritual genes of a poor self-image.

There is a very positive side to spiritual reproduction, like Mother Theresa for example who sowed love, compassion and humility whilst living in the slums of India and so what did Mother Theresa reproduce?

She reproduced thousands of men and women committed to this same vision all over the world and because she loved, she reproduced love. Kings and Presidents would greet this little lady from the slums with the red carpet treatment and bow to her as she walked into their presence.

I was sitting in the front row of the Sydney Entertainment Centre a couple of years ago attending a conference that included among the speakers General Norman H. Schwarzkopf and ex Russian President Mikhail Gorbachev.

As I looked around the room I saw some of the most influential leaders in Australia and something really struck me as a young man began his keynote speech, which he started by sharing his life's testimony.

When this young man was intending to leave school his careers officer called him into his office and told him that because he had a learning disability he should not expect to amount to anything special in life. He was told he should consider a job as a cleaner or something else of that nature, as this young man continued the room went totally silent and as I looked around at all the faces I sensed that many of the people in the room may have had a similar experience.

The words of death spoken by this young man's careers officer had a devastating effect on his life for several years and he felt so hopeless that he decided to search for THE KEY TO LIFE and after years of searching he said he finally found it.

Immediately the room went from quiet to an incredible silence, so silent in fact that it was almost noisy as everyone waited on the front of their seats for this young man to give them THE KEY TO LIFE.

He paused as he relived the past and then continued. "I read a book written in the 1920's by Dale Carnegie titled "HOW TO WIN FRIENDS AND INFLUENCE PEOPLE" and then he said, "Dale Carnegie invented THE KEY TO LIFE."

I sat in my seat looking around the room at the faces of hope and expectation as he made that incredible statement. It was one of those moments when you could see that almost everyone in the room was wearing their heart on their sleeve, because they desperately wanted him tell them THE KEY TO LIFE.

Another pause saw the anticipation rise to a new level and then he continued. "Dale Carnegie said... "AS A MAN THINKS IN HIS HEART SO IS HE."

The silence was replaced with a profound view of people pondering as they were digesting what he had just said. As I continued to look around the room I saw many people on the verge of tears and others with their heads in their hands as the power of this statement pierced their hearts.

At this point I was so tempted to jump to my feet and tell the real story about whom really made that statement but I managed to resist.

The young man had been incredibly impacted by what he read, but he got the punchline wrong. Dale Carnegie was an awesome man that pioneered motivational and public speaking, but he did not invent this statement and he certainly did not invent THE KEY TO LIFE and Mr. Carnegie never said that he did.

Dale Carnegie quoted a key of life, not THE KEY TO LIFE, and he quoted it from THE BOOK OF LIFE, the Bible which was written by THE AUTHOR OF LIFE. GOD!The Bible says,

> "*7 For as he thinks in his heart, so is he.*"
> Proverbs 23:7 (NKJ)

Great and awesome achievements come about by people believing in their hearts that they can do it and this young man applied the scripture to his life and at 23 years of age became a multi-millionaire.

THE LONG ARM OF THE LAW

The hunger to know THE KEY TO LIFE was apparent on many faces that day although many would think that these wealthy people had already found it, but money will never change the way you feel about yourself.

You will change the circumstances of your life and enjoy success and fulfilment in all that you do when you change the way you think about yourself. What you continually say to and about yourself together with the thoughts of your heart and mind will steer you in the direction you will go.

Positive words of affirmation spoken to yourself and to your circumstances will reproduce positive outcomes in your life, because the words you speak and the thoughts that you have also come under the law of reproduction. They have no choice but to reproduce <u>same species</u> or after their own kind.

Have a look around you for just a moment to see if you can see anything that was not created by words and you will not find anything, because everything that is, or ever will be was created in some way by words.

Paint it, design it, build it, manufacture it, sing it, mould it and on and on we could go, because God created everything including you and me and He is the Word.

> "[1]*In the beginning was the Word, and the Word was with God, and the Word was God. [2]He was with God in the beginning. [3]Through him all things were made; without him nothing was made that has been made.*"
> John 1:1-3

Start thinking positive thoughts and speaking positive words that will build you up then just watch the awesome changes that will take place in your life and your circumstances.

Everything will not change overnight because when you give birth to something there is always a time of conception, of pregnancy and then comes the birth. You are giving birth to a brand new way of thinking, speaking and acting which will result in you becoming a brand new person.

It took nine months for you to be born and you would not be here if you had given up, so make a decision right now to change the way you talk to yourself and to other people forever. Remember you were born a winner and you may mess up every single day, but just start again, because you will become stronger every day and because you are a winner you will never ever give up.

There are three types of people in our world, those who make it happen, those who watch it happen, and those who say, "what happened?"

Winners always make it happen, because they see things that are not, as though they have already happened. I have heard it said that out of the six or seven necessary skills that make up a champion golfer, such as sand save, putting, driving distance, driving distance accuracy, scrambling and pitching, Tiger Woods is not the number one in the world at any one of these particular skills, in fact it was said that he is not even in the top 10 at some of them.

Why is Tiger then the most incredible golfer in the world and will probably become the greatest golfer of all time? Tiger has the ability to clear his mind of all thoughts and interruptions and is able to visualise where the ball is going to land before he ever plays a shot, in other words he can see that which is not as though it were. Tiger is a master of focus and of calling or seeing those things that are not yet in the physical realm as if they already are and right there is the definition of faith. The dictionary meaning of faith is "trust or confidence in someone or something which is not based on proof."

The old saying, "SEEING IS BELIEVING" is in total opposition to faith because faith says, "NOT SEEING IS BELIEVING." The Bible says it this way.

> "*6And without faith it is impossible to please God, because anyone who comes to him must believe that he exists and that he rewards those who earnestly seek him.*"
> Hebrews 11:6

Tiger cannot see the result of the shot until he has played it, but he has faith and believes that the shot he has seen in his mind will come to pass and who can argue with his incredible record and the outcome of most of his shots?

Therefore have faith in the outcome of your commitment to change the thoughts that you think, the pictures you see and the words that you speak, so you will become a champion at life just like Tiger Woods is a champion at golf.

THE LAW OF SOWING AND REAPING

If I were to plant an orange tree in an orchard and diligently nurture it, by watering, fertilising and pruning it, in due season it will produce oranges.

If I was to go out into the orchard every day with a big stick and hit the orange tree for an hour, telling it never to produce oranges, but to produce water melons instead, I would be wasting my time and should seek instant medical help. The orange tree can only obey the universal law of reproduction and reproduce after it's own kind, in other words it will only ever reproduce <u>same species</u>.

The orange tree must submit to another universal law and that is the law of sowing and reaping. This law agrees with the law of reproduction and lets me know very clearly that whatever I sow I will reap and because I sowed an orange tree the fruit of my harvest or what I shall reap will be oranges, this harvest, next harvest and every harvest.

Not only does the law of sowing and reaping have a direct relationship with the law of reproduction, all the laws of the universe are designed to work in order and harmony with each other.

The law of sowing and reaping works in the unseen world just as it does in the seen world, because this law is a spiritual law and not a law that is made up by man.

We see and read about people every day that sow seed of one kind, but are expecting to reap a harvest of another kind; and this is never going to happen!

It does not matter in whose name or for what reason you sow something, because the law will not obey and reproduce after the name or the reason, but only after what has been sowed.

You cannot sow devastation, murder, rape, pillage and terror in the name of God or in the name of peace and expect to reap a harvest of anything else but exactly what you have sowed. The universal law of sowing and reaping does not listen to the reason that you sowed what you sowed; it only reproduces the <u>same species</u> and therefore if you do not like what you are harvesting or reaping then you must change the seed that you are sowing.

Another way we hear this law expressed is "what goes around comes around" which is just another way of saying, whatever you sow you shall reap and devastation seeds will reproduce a devastation harvest, just like orange trees produce orange harvests, pretty simple law isn't it?

The law of sowing and reaping works in conjunction with the law of the harvest and therefore you can sow something today but not get your harvest today or even tomorrow. When a child is conceived it is not born tomorrow and in fact it is not even apparent for some time that conception has even taken place, but rest assured the harvest is on its way and in due season it will be reaped.

Sometimes we see people appearing to reap the opposite to what they have sowed, they have been sowing good things and yet are reaping a life of turmoil and devastation, but if they do not give up and grow weary in doing good they will in due season reap exactly what they have sowed and so will you and I.

> "*9Let us not become weary in doing good, for at the proper time we will reap a harvest if we do not give up.*"
> Galatians 6:9

What we sow into our spirit, our soul and our body together with the actions and thoughts that we have will ultimately create or destroy our lives.

It's said that, "Sticks and stones will break my bones, but names

THE KEY TO LIFE

(words) will never hurt me."

This saying is one of the greatest lies ever told as we cannot count the number of people that have committed murder, suicide, genocide or live in depression and on the verge of suicide 24 hours a day because of the words of death and the abuse that they or other people have sowed into their lives.

I was watching a program on child abuse last night that took place here in Australia to young boy's that were placed in the care of an apparently safe and trustworthy organization. The terrible mental and physical abuse that many of these young boys had to suffer and endure still manifests itself in many of their lives today.

During the interviews it was very clear how dysfunctional many of these men were and to date some of them have committed suicide, some live on the street and others have locked themselves away as they trust no-one. Many of their marriages have broken down, as they feel hopeless, alone and without purpose. Some have admitted to having had the desire to or have even abused others because the very thing that was sowed into them as child has reproduced itself in them. We have the power to decide what will be reproduced in our lives and if we understand and apply these universal laws in a positive way we will reverse the affects of abuse and hopelessness. We must replace negative thinking and negative speaking with positive thinking and speaking words of life and not words of death.

CHANGE WORDS OF DEATH TO WORDS OF LIFE

- ✘ DEATH — You were a mistake.
- ⊷ LIFE — I was created on purpose for a purpose.

✘ DEATH — You will never make it.

⚿ LIFE — I will make it and achieve my dreams.

✘ DEATH — You're a loser.

⚿ LIFE — I was born a winner and will stay a winner.

✘ DEATH — You are ugly.

⚿ LIFE — I am a child of God and was created in his image.

✘ DEATH — You can't do it.

⚿ LIFE — I can, I can, and I will do it.

✘ DEATH — You are dumb.

⚿ LIFE — I have a gift and I intend to use it with all my heart.

✘ DEATH — You are useless.

⚿ LIFE — I am useful and I am successful.

✘ DEATH — I hate myself and other people.

⚿ LIFE — I love and respect myself because I am a child of God. I also love and care for the welfare of others because they are also God's children.

THE KEY TO LIFE

✘ DEATH — I want to die.

🗝 LIFE — I love life and I will live it to the fullest everyday.

✘ DEATH — I am fat.

🗝 LIFE — I am a disciplined person and I can lose weight when and if I choose. (Don't lose weight for other people do it when and if you feel you need to).

SOME IMPORTANT THINGS TO REMEMBER

- The most destructive habit — Worry
- The greatest joy — Giving
- The greatest loss — Loss of self-respect
- The most satisfying work — Helping others
- The ugliest personality trait — Selfishness
- The most endangered species — Dedicated leaders
- The greatest natural resource — You
- The greatest shot in the arm — Encouragement
- The greatest problem to overcome — Fear
- The most effective sleeping pill — Peace of mind
- The most crippling failure disease — Excuses

THE LONG ARM OF THE LAW

- The most powerful force in life — Love
- The most dangerous enemy — A gossiper
- The world's most incredible computer — The brain
- The worst thing to be without — Hope
- The deadliest weapon — The tongue
- The two most power-filled words — I can
- The greatest asset — Faith
- The most worthless emotion — Self-pity
- The most beautiful attire — A smile
- The most prized possession — Integrity
- The most powerful channel of communication — Prayer
- The most contagious spirit — Enthusiasm

Everyone, everywhere needs this list to live by!! When someone is hurt they often hurt others, but people that are healed, heal people.

The words "you are fat" have devastated millions of people down through history and that is one of the reasons why we have millions of male and female sufferers of Anorexia Nervosa and Bulimia in the world.

These people live in torment all day every day and I know this first hand as I suffered from Bulimia for 5 years. A man suffering from Bulimia you may be thinking, yes millions of them do and mine started with someone telling me that I was getting fat. I owned a gymnasium at the time and even teaching five aerobic classes a day would not keep the weight off, because I was also an alcoholic and would often drink 12 beers a day just to try and hide the pain that was in my heart, but the KEY TO LIFE set me free!

THE LAW OF AERODYNAMICS

Ironically I am writing this part of the book about the law of aerodynamics as I am flying from Sydney to Melbourne in Australia, it was not planned this way but what an appropriate time to do so.

As we taxi along the runway I am imagining as most people have, what I would do if an emergency arose and my life was about to end.

How these machines that weigh hundreds of tonnes get off the ground seemingly into nothing but fresh air is amazing, especially to the person who does not understand the law of aerodynamics, and these aircraft are only able to do what they do, as long as they obey the law of aerodynamics.

Obeying the law of aerodynamics allows the aircraft and its passengers to overcome the law of gravity, but the moment it ceases to obey, the law of gravity takes over and the aircraft will plunge toward the earth. Unless the pilot brings the aircraft back under the authority of the law of aerodynamics it will crash and all the passengers travelling with him will have to suffer, even though they did not personally break the law they become guilty by association.

These enormous aircraft are created on purpose, for a purpose and every part of them was created from the dust or ingredients of the ground. If the potential to create these giants of the air had not been sowed into the earth when it was created, then all those associated with aircraft manufacture could not have reached into the earth and reaped what had been already sowed thousands of years before. You cannot reap what is not sowed and you do not always have to be the sower to reap a harvest whether it be good or bad.

It is impossible to dig out of the earth what was not sown into it in the first place, because of the law of sowing and reaping. Once upon a time there were no aircraft and yet 500 or even 6,000 years ago, theoretically aircraft would have been able to fly then, just as they can today. All the ingredients were in the earth to make an aircraft and the law of aerodynamics was already operating so why did we not have any aircrafts?

Very simply no-one had built one, but then someone came along who had a dream and a vision in their heart and was prepared to pay the price to see what they had seen in the unseen world come into the seen world and the rest is history. That's what faith is; "... the substance of things hoped for and the evidence of things not seen." (Hebrews 11:1)

Walt Disney said, "If you can dream it, and believe it, you can achieve it, don't forget it all started with a mouse."

Every person has an element of faith on the inside because when you get on an aircraft or something similar you must have the faith that you will arrive at your destination or surely you would not get on it in the first place.

If you can have faith in something to arrive at its destination that you have absolutely no control of, then surely you can exercise faith in what you do have control of. That is faith in reaching your life goals, your purpose, your vision and your ultimate destination.

The pilots of aircrafts also have the faith that they will land at their desired destination or I am sure they would not have taken off in the first place.

Besides faith they also have something else that is critically important and which makes sure their faith is not just pie in the sky, excuse the pun.

The pilot has been given a flight plan and if he enters the flight plan data into the aircraft's flight management system he will arrive at his destination and if you enter your life plan into your life management system you will also arrive at your destination.

I understand that many of you may be in a situation that may not allow you to reach your desired destination and in fact you might be at the cross roads of your earthly life. If that is the case then there is a plan that will work within your current circumstances and that plan is to read this entire book so you can reach the same destination that was planned for every man, woman and child that has ever lived. As you continue page by page you will find out how to reach that destination and when you do, all that you could have had here on earth will pale to insignificance.

When the pilot obeys the law of sowing and reaping and sows the correct information into the flight management system he will reap the right destination and if he obeys the law of aerodynamics he will also land safely and the according to flight plan.

There is another universal law that says there can be no laws unless there is a law giver and that Law Giver has sowed a destination that

THE LONG ARM OF THE LAW

He is committed to for you to be able to reap.

ALTITUDE IS ALWAYS DETERMINED BY ATTITUDE

I arrived at the flying school in 1990 on Queensland's Gold Coast in Australia at 6.30 in the morning for my first lesson and after paying $115 for the hour, shook hands with the flying instructor, then walked with him to the aircraft without saying another word.

It was a magnificent day with not a single cloud in the sky and I was very nervous but also excited about this opportunity. As we taxied along the runway I listened and watched the instructor as he was observing and obeying all the instructions that were coming to him through his headphones from the control tower.

Within a couple of minutes we were airborne and still not another word had been spoken to me by the instructor, so I just continued to observe all that he was doing.

When we got to 1,500 feet the first words that came out of the instructors mouth were, "OK, Nigel, now the first thing I want you to do is to get your attitude right."

I was very taken back by his statement and actually thought, how rude. I had not spoken a word to him apart from good morning and so I could not work out why he would speak to me like that.

He didn't even know me and I was the customer who had just separated with $115, which in 1990 was quite significant for an hours flying lesson. I gathered my thoughts before I spoke, because at 1,500 feet with nowhere to go to say I am out of here was not appropriate and so I said calmly "what do you mean, 'get my attitude right?'"

THE KEY TO LIFE

This was all part of his student flight plan because he smiled and started to explain what he meant by saying for me to get my attitude right.

He explained that when you fly this particular single engine aircraft you put your hand on its edge, with the little finger on the dashboard and then line up the horizon by looking across the first finger of your hand. If you are having difficulties picturing this, put your left hand in front of your face with your palm facing you, now look across your first finger and line it up with an object in the distance, have you got it?

Once you have lined the two up you know that you are flying up the right way, which is a great idea and also that you are flying straight and level, which is also a great idea.

Once you are at the right altitude, all you have to do is slightly adjust what is called the trim wheel with your other hand and you feel the aircraft slip into an invisible slot.

It is an amazing sensation when this happens because you can take your hands off the controls and the aircraft will fly straight and level all on its own, so this is what he meant when he said to get my attitude right.

When you can take your hands off the controls it means your angle of attack or your attitude to the horizon is right, and in your life it means that your attitude to your destination, your goals, your vision and your destination is right.

The instructor then said something that blew my mind, however I am not sure whether he knew the impact of what he had said or even whether he had ever experienced the same revelation.

THE LONG ARM OF THE LAW

He said "Nigel, your attitude will always determine your altitude." Then he said if you put the nose of the aircraft down, your attitude will decrease and if you put the nose of the aircraft up your attitude will increase.

This law of aerodynamics that operates for an aircraft also operates in your life, because when your nose is down your attitude is down and when your nose is up your attitude goes up and so does your altitude. Anytime you lose your attitude you also lose your altitude and if your attitude stays that way for too long you will crash land just like the aircraft would. Your angle of attack will change your attitude and your nose will stop pointing to the ground, so that once again you will be able to see the horizon which is your goal in front of you, and then you will climb to new and higher levels.

Large aircraft choose to fly at around 30,000 to 36,000 feet because that is where they perform at their best and at that incredible height the mountains and the valleys look very insignificant. I encourage you to be like the pilot and to get above your circumstances and look down on them from a great altitude, with a great attitude and you will see many of them as insignificant.

Please do not read me wrong here because many of you have circumstances that are overwhelming and I am not making small of that, but I want to bring perspective into your every day battles which can be overcome with the right attitude.

The pilot is in control of the attitude and therefore the altitude of the aircraft and that small voice from the control tower that comes through the head phones can only guide and suggest what the pilot should do, but at the end of the day he has to make the decision about what he actually does.

THE KEY TO LIFE

You are at the controls of your life and there is a small voice that seeks to speak to you, of whom you read about later, but at the end of the day the decision to tune into that voice and obey it is yours.

There are many voices that are trying to speak to us all the time and we are all very familiar with them. You know the voice that gives you a thought to do something wrong and then you hear the voice of integrity saying to you, no don't do it.

We have a decision to make right at that moment as to whether we are going to obey the voice of protection and integrity or the voice of deception and eventual destruction.

Many times just like an aircraft the sun will go down on you and you may fall into the deepest of darkness, but the great news is that after the darkest hour of the night comes the sunrise. When your attitude and your altitude are in right relationship to the horizon you will be able to see the sun rise on you again. Hang in there and get your attitude in line with the horizon because the sun will rise again and in fact THE SON is about to rise in your life.

What does an aircraft do when there is darkness and storms all around and the pilot cannot even see the horizon?

Planes have a horizon built into their dashboard when they are created for this very reason and so it makes no difference whether it is dark or stormy, it does not affect their ability to fly through the darkness or through stormy weather.

Pilots can fly without being able to see where they are physically going because their vision is not affected by the fact that they cannot see anything.

They have a plan and so they not only know where they came from but they also know very clearly where they are going. Rain, hail or snow will not stop them from arriving at their pre-determined destination even though on some occasions they may have to take a detour and perhaps even land somewhere other than their intended destination for a time, but in due course they know that they will arrive safely at their original destination and so will you.

You were also created with an inbuilt horizon that will allow you to see when you can't see, it will show you whether you are flying straight and level, climbing or descending and it will allow you to keep on going toward your vision even though you seem to be flying blind.

You also may need to take the occasional detour and even land somewhere other than your desired destination for a while. This is the time to refuel and take a breather, so that you will be refreshed and ready to once again take off towards your vision and your ultimate destination.

If you do not have a plan or a destination in mind then you are likely to crash land every time you take off, but if you do have a plan and you are right in the middle of a storm with your attitude right, your altitude right and your internal horizon set, you will be flying straight and level towards your destiny.

Darkness may temporarily envelop you and you see no hope and no light at the end of the tunnel, but keep your eyes on the horizon because you will see the light and feel the warmth of the sun even before it rises on you again.

For exercise I love to run because of the adrenalin high and mostly

I run at our local Olympic training track because it is all marked out, which helps me to set my training goals.

One day while I was running I had a very powerful revelation which I want to share it with you because it is very relevant to losing sight of your vision and your goals when you stop moving toward them.

I was running this particular day with my sunglasses on and having just completed my laps, was finishing off by running some 100 metre sprints.

At 49 years of age many would think I was exaggerating by saying I was sprinting the 100 metres and they are probably right, but I felt the pain of every one of them.

I was very hot from running so at the end of each 100 metres I would take a breather before running the next and I would turn my back on the track, walk around for a while to gather my breath so I could continue.

This walking around caused my eyes to be temporarily taken off the track, which was my goal and I noticed that each time I stopped running my sunglasses would fog up. Because my glasses were now fogged up I had no vision at all and I could not even see a foot in front of myself.

Once I refocussed on the track for my next 100 and then actually starting running again towards my next goal, the fog evaporated immediately from my sunglasses and my vision was once again very clear, allowing me to see the goal in front of me.

That was an amazing revelation that taught me not to stop running toward my goal when my vision was fogged up, impaired, or even lost all together when I was taking a breather or had been beaten up by some circumstance in my life.

I learned that my vision and my goals were still there even though I could not see them with my natural eye and all I had to do, was the same as the pilot does, trust my internal instrument panel and get running once again so that the vision would reappear.

It is important to take a breather from time to time and also realise that you will be beaten up and challenged on your way to your vision, because success will fight you all the way.

Check your internal instrument panel, refocus on your goals, then get up, get going and once again your vision will become as clear as it was the day you got it.

Start running with purpose, forward momentum and unconditional commitment toward your vision and it will be well within your grasp.

Last night I watched Anthony "The Man" Mundine fight for and win the World Super Middle Weight Boxing Title, which was an incredible effort because only three years ago Anthony was not boxing, but was a champion rugby league player.

Many players have gone from rugby league to rugby union and vice versa, but to go from rugby league to the World Boxing Champion in just three years is incredible, but there are very good reasons why Anthony became World Champion.

When Anthony finished his Rugby League career he made a statement for the entire world to hear. He said words to the effect of....,

"I will become World Boxing Champion."

Many people thought that Anthony was just being a big mouth and yet they did not realise that Anthony had thought hard and long about the price he would have to pay to become World Champion. Not only was he prepared to pay the price but he was totally committed to his vision, his goals and he designed a plan with very specific time frames to achieve his goal.

By sharing his vision in the public arena he was casting it before the people, knowing that some would catch his vision and run with him and that others who were not for him would try to destroy the seed that he had so boldly sowed.

Anthony is one of those very special people who lives to achieve things that supposedly can't be done and when he is told it can't be done, he goes out and does it.

Anthony knew very well what he sowed would bring a harvest of negativity and verbal attack, but that is exactly the harvest he wanted to reap because it was the very fuel he needed to inspire and motivate him to become World Champion.

Anthony may not yet know that he was born a winner and can die a winner, but he certainly knows that he can live a winner.

> "THOSE WHO SAY IT CAN'T BE DONE SHOULDN'T INTERRUPT THOSE WHO ARE DOING IT"

CHAPTER FIVE
WORDS ARE YOUR BEST FRIEND OR YOUR WORST ENEMY

> "*¹In the beginning was the Word, and the Word was with God, and the Word was God. ²He was with God in the beginning. ³Through Him all things were made; without Him nothing was made that has been made. ⁴In Him was life and that life was the light of men.*"
> John 1:1-4

This awesome Scripture from the Bible summarises not only the power of God but the power of words, whether they are word pictures, words that are thought, sign language or the incredible power of the spoken word.

Nothing has ever been or will ever be created without words because words are the force behind all creation and they give us the incredible ability and power to create something out of nothing.

The Jumbo Jet, the Motor Vehicle, the Pyramids and all other achievements created by mankind had their beginning with the spoken word and every part of them came from the dust of the ground.

Imagine planning and then creating the Jumbo Jet without a word being spoken, I can see the engineering team now all looking at each other and waiting for something to happen.

Try it yourself for a couple of hours, say nothing, write nothing, no sign language, no body language, show absolutely no form of communication whatsoever and see how much you get done.

Words are the foundation to the creation of the entire universe because God said I am the Word, and so when He created the heavens, the earth and all that is in it, He spoke or sowed His Word, then it came to pass.

The Bible says in the book of Genesis that God created man from the dust of the earth and to check this out, take a sample of your skin to a pathology lab and have it analysed.

You will find that your skin has the same basic elements as those that are found in the dust of the ground, which is no surprise because God said in His Word.

> "*26 Then God said, 'Let us make man in our image, in our likeness, and let them rule over the fish of the sea and the birds of the air, over the livestock, over all the earth, and over all the creatures that move along the ground.' 27 So God created man in his own image, in the image of*

> *God he created him; male and female he created them."*
> Genesis 1:26-27

Words have the ability to create or to destroy and words have caused millions of people, in fact entire nations to perish right throughout history. Man's arguments over written and spoken words are the basis of much of the incredible devastation that we see in our world today.

Just as God's Word created the physical world that we live in, your words will create or destroy the world that you live in.

To change your life, circumstances, opportunities and destiny you must change the words you think, you listen to and also the words that you speak.

With your words you can build trust, relationships, people, and business empires, but with your words you can also destroy these things as well.

Have you ever noticed that bitter and sweet waters sometimes come out of the same fountain, the fountain being our mouth? This tiny little member of our body has the power to transform lives and entire nations for good or for evil, but the decision as to which path we will take is entirely ours.

HOW WORDS CREATE OR DESTROY

The Bible says,

> *"²¹The tongue has the power of life and death, and those who love it will eat its fruit."* Proverbs 18:21

Mr. Ray Kroc was the man recognized for creating the McDonalds Hamburger Empire. In 1961 Kroc approached the McDonald brothers and offered to buy them out. They agreed and he paid them $2.7 million and then by 1966 there were 800 restaurants. (Kroc claimed that there were only 8 failures in the first 11 years McDonalds was opened.) Gross revenue was about $35 million (although many people have heard higher figures) and then the company went public on the New York Stock Exchange.

Two thousand dollars ($2,000) worth of stock bought in those early days is worth about $3 million today and in 1966 there were still just 10 items on the menu, none costing over 29 cents.

- Hamburgers — 15 cents

- Milk Shakes — 25 cents

- Soft Drinks — 10 and 15 cents

- Fish Sandwich — 29 cents

In the late 1960s, McDonalds began to widen menu options, introducing the "Big Mac" in 1968 and then in conjunction with its Big Breakfast push, introduced the Egg McMuffin in 1973.

Kroc was also known to be a big stickler for cleanliness and one of his more famous sayings was, "If you have time to lean, you have time to clean." Parents try this on your children.

By 1980, there were 6,500 outlets with revenue of $6.2 billion. By then, Kroc was making more on real estate deals and finding locations for the restaurants than he was from franchise fees and as he spread his operation overseas McDonalds was fast becoming a symbol of American business around the world.

McDonalds also became an important stepping stone for Americans entering the labour force and the company claimed in 1998 that 1 in every 8 Americans had worked, or did work for them.

Today McDonalds has about 30,000 restaurants and more than $40 billion in sales, with franchises in 120 countries. If they had only opened one new restaurant every day it would have taken a staggering 82 years to open the 30,000 stores. This not only shows us the power of the word, but also the incredible power of a vision.

Mr. Kroc probably approached the McDonald brothers and made them an offer either by the written word or the spoken word. With that offer and those words Mr. Kroc created an opportunity to fulfil his vision, he communicated his vision, his dream and his plan and the rest is history.

It was the words that he thought, he wrote and spoke that allowed him to build the business that today is worth billions of dollars and it all started with the power of a vision and the power of words.

If the words Mr. Kroc used with his financiers, his employees and his customers were inappropriate there would be no McDonalds, because the words he spoke would have destroyed his vision before it even got started.

What about the words you speak to yourself, these are the words that will build or destroy your life and also the people that are around you. If you listen and convince yourself of the words behind some wrong perception you may have, you will make that perception a reality, because of the law of sowing and reaping.

WORDS ARE YOUR BEST FRIEND OR YOUR WORST ENEMY

You may keep telling yourself that people don't like you and yet the truth might be that many people enjoy your company and want to be your friend, but your negative opinion of yourself drives them away and destroys any relationship you may have had.

The words you speak to yourself will determine how you will deal with challenges in life and where you will end up at the end of this human race. The words that others speak to you are just as powerful and you may have experienced the following words spoken to you as a little child. You were a mistake, you were an accident, you will never amount to anything, you are a failure, we are going to put you in a foster home, you are too much and we don't want anymore.

Many people have suffered terrible verbal abuse since early childhood and now they believe the words that were spoken into their lives. I encourage you not to speak about the abuse and the mountains of resistance that have or will come against you when in the pursuit of your vision and goals, but get somewhere on your own and speak to them like this.

"You may think you that you are going to stop me, but I will defeat you and I will win. I might need to climb you, go around you, or just maybe I will go straight through you and so get out of my way because I am coming through."

The words that you speak into the atmosphere around your life, known in the Bible as speaking into the spirit realm, have the same creative or destructive power as when they are spoken to another person or yourself, so go ahead and watch some awesome changes happen.

THE KEY TO LIFE

Peter J. Daniels is one Australia's very motivated men and also one of the world's most successful leadership and motivational speakers. His clients include such people as President Nelson Mandela and yet when Peter was a schoolboy his teacher Miss Phillips told him that he was a bad, bad boy and he would never amount to anything. The last time I spoke with Peter he had just been paid a consultancy fee of one million dollars, not bad, for a bad, bad boy.

Peter has written several best selling books including one titled "Miss Phillips You Were Wrong." In this book he writes how Miss Phillip's words of death had a very negative and devastating effect on his life, so he went in search of, what makes the great, great!

He desperately wanted to find out what makes the great, great and so he spent many years reading (in his own words) around 5,000 biographies of the most successful people in history, only to find out what makes the great, great, was already written in the Bible. Now having finally found what makes the great, great, Peter also found THE KEY TO LIFE.

The Bible refers to what Jesus said and did when He knew his life vision and purpose was to die on a cross for you and me.

> "*7Because the Sovereign LORD helps me, I will not be disgraced. Therefore have I set my face like flint, and I know I will not be put to shame. 8He who vindicates me is near. Who then will bring charges against me? Let us face each other! Who is my accuser? Let him confront me! 9It is the Sovereign LORD who helps me. Who is he that will condemn me? They will all wear out like a garment; the moths will eat them up. 10Who among you fears the LORD and obeys the word of his servant? Let him who walks in the dark, who has no light, trust in the name of*

> *the LORD and rely on his God."*
> Isaiah 50:7-10

Jesus knew his vision, mission, goal and purpose on earth was to go to the cross and be crucified for our sins. I have underlined the key words in this scripture because they are paramount to you achieving your vision, your mission, your goals, your purpose and your destiny.

Jesus set His face like a flint towards His destiny, knowing full well what He would have to endure to reach the goal and He never lost sight of it until it was finished.

> "*[30]When he had received the drink, Jesus said, 'It is finished.' With that, he bowed his head and gave up his spirit.*"
> John 19:30

He took the penalty for the sin of the world on His shoulders and was crucified knowing that this was the only way He could overcome God's law of sin and death. He knew that His death would overcome the law and would open the way for you and me to have eternal life with Him in Heaven.

In a ministry that lasted just three years Jesus achieved what we could never achieve and one example is when he died on the cross the entire time and date system on planet earth was split it in two. This same splitting in two happened to a three feet thick curtain that was in the Tabernacle not far from where he was crucified and it happened the very moment that Jesus took his last breath and now whenever we write the date we authenticate that Jesus walked on earth.

A date in our day written in full will read like this, the 11th day of May 2004 AD.

What does the "AD" part mean? In Latin it is written "Anno Domini", which means in the year of our Lord, the Lord Jesus Christ, however many have been taught or just know it as "AD" or AFTER THE DEATH OF CHRIST.

There is some confusion amongst historians as to the exact dates of the initials "BC" which in Latin used to be "AC" or "Ante Christum" but there is absolutely no confusion as to what "AC" or "BC" means, as they both mean and authenticate the very same thing and that is before the birth of Jesus Christ or BEFORE CHRIST.

Have you ever stopped to think why we would use the time and date system of BC or AD, if in fact Jesus never existed? There are many groups right now as we speak who are trying to change our time and date system to CE (Common Era) and BCE (Before the Common Era). Here is a brief edited outline of the reason why from one of the websites.

"The golden rule suggests that one should not intentionally cause pain to other humans and we should treat others as we would wish to be treated. Since only one in every three humans on earth is a Christian some theologians and other authors felt that non-religious neutral terms like CE and BCE would be less offensive to the non Christian majority. Forcing a non Christian to use AD and BC might be seen by some as coercing them to acknowledge the supremacy of the Christian God and of Jesus Christ.

They are right we should treat other humans with incredible dignity and respect, but let me assure you if God has to offend us to get our attention so that we will receive His Son Jesus Christ as our Lord and Saviour, so we can receive eternal life He will do it. The reason He will do it is because He loves us so much and He wants to get us out of satan's kingdom and into His Kingdom. Satan is your arch enemy and he would love to destroy your belief in anything to do with Jesus Christ and he is the motivator of this rubbish. When the name if Jesus is preached the law of Heaven says that satan must bow his knee and when Jesus returns, satan goes to hell where he belongs.

Millions of people have been sold the lie that Jesus is just a fairy tale, like Santa Claus and the Easter Bunny or believe that He hasn't come yet and if that is the case then we are all living in a made up fantasy world, so lets get out of here. Seriously, why would anyone consider naming planet earth's time and date system after someone who never even existed or has not even come here yet, this is not Fantasy Island or The Wizard of Oz, this is your life we are talking about and there is no video replay.

Jesus Himself said the following in the Gospel of John;

> "¹⁶*For God so loved the world that he gave his one and only Son, that whoever believes in him shall not perish but have eternal life."*
> John 3:16

Set your face like a flint towards your vision, your goal and your destiny.

A flint is a very hard piece of rock or stone and if your face is set in one direction like a rock you cannot look to the left or to the right and therefore be persuaded by everyone and everything that seeks to rob you of your vision.

Reading those words in the Bible that day and then applying them to his life changed Peter J. Daniel's forever and will also change you forever.

When you speak words of life and make promises to yourself that you intend to keep like "I will, I can do this, I will work hard to achieve my goals, I will never give up, tomorrow is a new day, I will do my best every time, I have the talent to fulfil my chosen purpose or career," awesome things will begin to happen for you, now here is another great testimony to encourage you.

Kieren Perkins to date is Australia's greatest ever 800 and 1500 metre swimmer and is still a World Record Holder, winning Gold Medals at the Olympic Games in 1992 and 1996. Here is an interview with Kieren.

His technically perfect Olympic Gold Medal winning performances at Atlanta and Barcelona over 1500 metres have become historic moments in Australian sport. In a country where sport is a part of our culture, Kieren's success earns him a place alongside heroes like Dawn Fraser and Sir Donald Bradman.

Kieren: "You have to have goals and you have to have things you want to achieve."

But Kieren's success today is a long way from the days when he first took up the sport.

Born in Brisbane in 1973, Kieren and his younger brother were encouraged by their parents to participate in sport.

Kieren: "Dad had a policy and that was, we had to do a sport, my brother and I, it didn't matter what it was but we had to do a sport and they would support us in that."

After trying soccer, football and swimming, Kieren decided he liked the water best, but swimming became more than just a past-time when, at the age of nine, he fell through a plate glass door and severed his calf muscle.

He didn't know it at the time, but that accident was to have a big influence on the rest of his life, because Doctors suggested swimming as a way of strengthening his leg.

It was at the local pool where Kieren met his swimming coach John Carew, who would have a big influence on his swimming success.

Kieren: "The main role of a coach is firstly to teach the kids how to swim properly, then secondly to train them and make sure that they do the work and that they train hard."

Even in the early stages of his swimming career, Kieren had to strive to improve.

Kieren: "When I was young my main motivating thing was I had to improve, I had to do my personal best time. When I was in primary school, probably no more than ten or eleven years old, I'd just come last in this race by you know a couple of metres and I jumped out of the pool and ran into the stand with a huge grin on my face and all I said to Mum and Dad was you know, "Is that my best time, did I do my best time? and that's been my philosophy, it's been what's driven me from when I was that young right up until now, it's still the standard that I use, have I done my best?"

During these early years, swimming was fun but schoolwork at Brisbane Boys' College took up most of his time.

Kieren: "Right throughout my childhood I guess I always recognized that schooling was a very important thing and swimming wouldn't last forever and so I did work reasonably hard at school.

Then at age fifteen Kieren began to win some races.

Kieren: "The time that I did decide I was going to make swimming I guess a profession was when I was fifteen and I won my first State Title and then went on to the Nationals and won my first National Title and that was the time when I did start to, I guess show a bit of talent."

Kieren started training full time, he was swimming around seventy kilometres per week at training sessions before and after school.

Kieren focussed on his goal with fierce determination and trained himself to never give up.

Kieren: "One of the things that I learned right from when I was young because I was never very talented and I never won many races that I learnt that tomorrow's a new day you know, you will have another chance and one of the things that you really do have to believe is that just because today's gone bad doesn't mean next time's going to be bad. You've got to work hard to achieve your goals and you know never give up, because the people who give up are the people who don't achieve."

In 1990 he began breaking world records in the four hundred, eight hundred and fifteen hundred metre events at the World Championships and Commonwealth Games. His record—breaking performances made him the greatest distance swimmer in the world and have redefined human ability in long distance swimming.

Kieren: "I guess in the last five or six years when you know I've broken World Records and won Olympic Gold Medals, a lot of those races you know I've won by five, ten, fifteen, twenty seconds and to be in that situation you're not racing anybody else but yourself and I always have raced myself, I've always wanted to get the best out of myself and do my best. We all have a talent, we all have the ability to be good at something and it's not always sport, you know it can be in business, it can be in science and you know at school. Whatever it is, we do all have the ability to be good at something."

END OF INTERVIEW

I have heard it said that during another interview when asked what was it like to be the greatest ever 1500 metre swimmer of all time and be to a Gold Medallist at 19 years of age Kieren said, "I didn't win it when I was 19, I won it when I was 8 as I saw this moment every time I swam up and down the pool at training."

What an incredible statement to make especially from such a young boy.

Right there is the Bible definition of faith, "Seeing things that are not as though they are."

I have a daily affirmations list which I keep in my briefcase and I read it out loud to myself everyday, because I have to remind myself on a daily basis to focus on my vision and goals.

THE KEY TO LIFE

I know that as I speak these affirmations to myself I am watering the seed that I sowed when I established my vision and these positive, prayerful words overcome the negative thoughts that always seek to steal.

We live in a very negative world and being negative can have power over being positive because it requires little or no action, but just like darkness cannot exist when you turn the light on, negativity can't exist when you are being positive.

If we do not like what we are reaping then it is very simple, we must change what we are sowing. Modern medicine is finally learning the power of words and it is now accepted that speaking negative words creates physical changes take place in us and these changes can lead to illness. A medical survey undertaken to establish whether prayer would assist in the healing process of people in hospital showed without doubt, that those who had been prayed for recovered markedly quicker than those who did not get prayed for.

Prayer is words being prayed to God in the name of Jesus who is the greatest Doctor and Healer of all and so with Him on your side great things will happen when you speak positive words into your life. Never come down to the mentality of the crowd, you must encourage them to rise up and discover a life full of hope, joy and fulfilment.

The point about words is simple, you need to take them seriously because they will create or destroy your life.

Become a tradesperson with the words that you speak, just like there are Blacksmiths and Goldsmiths, both of whom are experts in their fields of endeavour you need to become a Wordsmith.

A Wordsmith is a person who creates life, purpose and hope with the words they speak and their finished product becomes something of great value.

THE POWER OF WORD PICTURES

It has been said that by the time we are thirty years of age we have an internal mental library of more than 3,000,000 negative and positive pictures that we can draw on.

Have you ever listened to a storyteller and seen exactly what they are talking about in your mind or listened to a radio play, a talking book or a lecture tape and seen exactly what was being spoken about?

As you have been reading this book you would have read some words and then seen a picture in your mind's eye, these word pictures that you see have the power in them to shape and determine the direction of your life.

Most of the great motivational and life changing speakers of our time stress the importance of daily affirmations and prayer, they emphasise how positive affirmations and prayer help to direct our lives. This need not take hours to achieve each day, but the way you start your day is most often also how you will finish it.

You will still have many challenges on a day to day basis but you will know how to speak to them and pray about them, rather than allowing them to defeat you.

CHAPTER SIX
HOW TO GET A VISION
AND THEN SEE IT TO FRUITION

WHAT IS VISION?

"The act or power of perceiving what is not actually present to the eye." The Pocket Macquarie Dictaurus

The Bible says that without a vision people perish. Millions of people around the world are trying to find the answers in drugs, alcohol, sex, fame and money. If drugs were THE KEY TO LIFE, then drug addicts should be the happiest people on earth but they are not. If alcohol was THE KEY TO LIFE, then alcoholics should be the happiest people on earth but they are not and if sex was THE KEY TO LIFE, then prostitutes should be the happiest people on earth and they are not. If fame and money was THE KEY TO LIFE, then the rich and famous should be the happiest people on earth and I have met and read about many that are amongst the unhappiest people on the face of the earth.

The photographer from the movie THE PASSION OF THE CHRIST is a man by the name of Ken Duncan and he not only did the photography for the movie but also is a very good friend of the movie's creator and director Mel Gibson. Ken has now produced a best selling book called THE PASSION that has all the photographs from the movie in it. I encourage you to buy this awesome book as Mel himself wrote the forward in the book and talks about how depressed he was until he found THE KEY TO LIFE.

Ken Duncan was speaking at our Church recently and shared a story about Mel, with his full knowledge and permission.

Ken's story about Mel went something like this…! Mel said he was standing on the 14th floor of a New York hotel and was so depressed that he considered jumping off. He said that everyone else seemed to be enjoying and celebrating his success except for himself. As he considered jumping thoughts of the Bible went through his mind and so he thought if I commit suicide and there is a hell I might just end up there.

Mel in his desperation cried out to God to help him and all of a sudden a peace descended upon him that was beyond his normal understanding. This is not surprising because the Bible says that this very thing will happen as Jesus said.

> "28 *Come to me, all you who are weary and burdened, and I will give you rest."*
> Matthew 11:28

THE KEY TO LIFE

THE PASSION OF THE CHRIST movie is a huge box office success and the vision to create it was birthed in Mel out of the experience he had with God on the 14th floor of that New York hotel.

Within a couple of days of his experience with God, Mel visited a library and as he walked along the rows a book fell out of a shelf. Mel picked it up and put it back on the shelf and walked on, the same book once again fell from the shelf and so he turned back, picked it up and put it back, then walked on. For some amazing reason as he walked away it fell out of the shelf again and this time he not only picked it up but had an urgency to open it.

It opened to a page where a Christian lady was talking about the incredible passion that Jesus Christ had to die for us and right there at that very moment Mel Gibson had the vision for THE PASSION OF THE CHRIST movie birthed in him. This same vision impartation miracle from God has happened to me and millions and millions of other people and it can also happen to you.

Mel Gibson is one of the finest actors of all time and reportedly invested around $30,000,000 of his own money into this movie. I saw a home video of Mel thanking Christians around the world for their prayers, as every resistance and conflict you could imagine was unleashed against him when he was trying to do his movie. Mel said something like, "I don't care what happens to me because I now know why I have been put on this earth and that is to show people everywhere what Jesus Christ the Messiah did for them when He died on the cross."

Mel played two parts in his movie and when he told that to a reporter, the reporter said that he did not see him and so which parts did he play? This is what Mel said about just one of the parts he played, it is a scene where you can only see his arm, as he held the nail steady before it was driven into Jesus' hand on the cross.

The reporter asked why he had invested so much of his own money in this movie and yet only played such an insignificant role. Mel said it certainly was not insignificant and chose to play that part because he realised that it was his own sin that nailed Jesus to the cross. WOW!!!!

How could Mel Gibson be depressed with his money and all his fame you might ask? Money and fame is never the answer and they often lead to a 'if it feels good, then do it' mindset. They can lead to a life without boundaries, where drugs, alcohol and the like begin to take control your life and these things always promise so much, but they never deliver on their promises, leading to devastated, broken lives.

The happiest people on earth are those who have found THE KEY TO LIFE, because when you have found it you will have vision, purpose and an eternal destiny to look forward to.

I have met many wealthy people, sporting champions, great actors and entertainers and many other successful people as measured by the world standards who feel very lost and very alone. Often their marriages are a mess or have fallen apart, their children don't want to know them and others are addicted and feel like complete losers. They drink or take drugs to hide the pain in their hearts, but these things do not hide the pain for very long, as the next day the pain comes out of its hiding place.

Just recently, and it happens hundreds of times a day across the world,

I saw on television several very high profile actors and actresses in the USA that had admitted themselves into dry out clinics for drugs and alcohol and why would they do this if these things were THE KEY TO LIFE. I can relate to these people and that is why I am writing this book, I was an alcoholic with no vision, no hope and no future and so I drank to hide the pain, but there is an answer, there is a hope and there is a destiny.

A vision is a very clear picture of your future and destiny that will work like a magnet in your daily life and draw you towards it. I said it before and will probably say it again because 10 years as a sales trainer has taught me that repetition is a major key to learning. You must fight for success because it will fight against you, whereas negativity will fight for you, it requires no effort because you just sit around and pull everyone and everything down.

You fought like a lion to get here, so you have the stuff already in you to fight for your vision, your dreams and your destiny. God knew that you would have to fight the good fight to achieve anything in life, so maybe that is why you had so much resistance in the form of millions of competitors all racing against you to get here in the first place.

If there is no real chance that you can fail then where is the power in victory and if you cannot lose then where is the joy in winning. What we think about most of the time is what we will be drawn to and once again that is the law of sowing and reaping in action.

When I am sales training I teach salespeople among other things how to qualify the customer by finding out their number one priority in considering the salesperson's product or service. Once the salesperson has the customer's number one priority, they also have their number one buying motive and should then design the presentation or the demonstration around the customer's DBM (Dominant Buying Motive), in other words around the customer's vision for the product or services ability to fulfil their needs.

Don't let anyone else design your vision, your goals and your destiny for you, because when they do they will always make them too small and then also want all the glory if you succeed.

THE DREAMS / VISION VALUE FORMULA

"When the perceived value of your vision and your dream in your heart exceeds the price you will have to pay to achieve it, your vision and dream will become a reality."

If this life appears to be over for you either medically or for some other reason, I understand this chapter is difficult for you but there is great news to come, so please keep reading.

A few years ago I was an average salesman and in fact it was worse than that, I felt like a bit of a con man because I did not believe that selling was a honourable profession. Then one night at Church a visiting preacher said something very simple and yet it impacted me greatly.

He said, "Whatever gifts you have they are from God, if you are a gifted carpenter then become the best carpenter you can and if you are a gifted salesperson then become the best salesperson you can."

I no longer felt like a con man because I realised that my gift was selling and I could sell with integrity, so that very night I made a commitment to be the best salesman I could and when I made that commitment my whole life turned around, so did my opportunities.

I had tried many things in my life and paid the price for having no vision or purpose, but now that I have both, I am focussed when I get up in the morning and excited because I know where I am heading. I am totally committed to helping you change your life so can we get committed together, is it a deal?

Your vision should be realistic and achievable and if it is motivated by good you can change the world that you live in. Nelson Mandela's vision saw him face 27 years in jail for what he believed in and then he became the President of his Nation and in his late 80's is still daily serving people.

Negative visions are just as powerful, Hitler's vision destroyed millions of lives, where Mother Theresa's vision although she is now in Heaven continues to feed and bring restoration to millions of lives.

If you don't have a vision for your life, then there is not much point in living and so get a vision, to find a vision.

I heard many people over many years talking about the need to have a goal, a dream, a purpose and a vision for my life, but nobody actually explained to me what a vision was, how I could get one and how I could make it come to pass when I did get one, so I had to find out for myself. We will talk a lot about universal laws throughout this book because you will see shortly how obeying just one of these laws will guarantee you fulfil your life purpose and destiny.

Finding a vision was a time of deep inner searching and so I asked myself this question, if I could do whatever I wanted to do what would that be? I removed all the obstacles such as money, geography, time, ability, education, distance and anything else that would hinder my dream machine from searching my heart.

I finally realised that beyond everything else I could choose to do, one thing stood out and that was the burning desire in my heart to bring hope where there was none and to introduce people to a transformed life and the only way I could do that was to help them find THE KEY TO LIFE.

I wanted to help people become all that God created them to be and to inspire those who are in situations that may not allow them to fulfil their earthly dreams and that being the case, how they can make an eternal difference to themselves and others right where they are now, it has taken 20 years of preparation but that is what I am doing now.

Preparation is a prerequisite to helping others to achieve, because you can only ever successfully sow into other peoples lives that which has not only been sown into your life, but that you have victory over.

When you have finished reading this chapter I encourage you put the book down, sit back, close your eyes and ask yourself and God to help you establish a vision for your life.

Be patient because in time the thoughts, the pictures and the dreams will come rushing into your mind and so start writing them all down, don't cast any of them out until you are finished scanning through them all.

You will be calling on many of the millions of pictures that are stored in the filing cabinet of your heart and mind. When you get the one that sets you on fire, work with it until it becomes part of you and be prepared to ask God to help you, because He says in His Word that He has a plan for your life.

> "*[11] For I know the plans I have for you,*" *declares the LORD, "plans to prosper you and not to harm you, plans to give you hope and a future."*
> Jeremiah 29:11

> "*[5] Trust in the LORD with all your heart and lean not on your own understanding; [6] in all your ways acknowledge Him, and He will make your paths straight."*
> Proverbs 3:5-6

> "*[13] For you created my inmost being; you knit me together in my mother's womb. Your eyes saw my unformed body. All the days ordained for me were written in Your book before one of them came to be."*
> Proverbs 139:13

There is a story about Helen Keller, the blind, deaf American woman who learned to speak and became a world famous lecturer and author. Helen received many awards and diplomas and in 1955 won an Oscar Award for the documentary film "Helen Keller in Her Story." This remarkable woman although blind could see more than many of those who could see and when asked what would be worse than being blind, she reportedly answered, "Being able to see without a vision."

Helen also said the following. "The unhappiest people in the world are those who have sight, but have no vision."

THOUGHTS ABOUT VISION!

VISION — is birthed firstly in the darkroom of your heart and then screened in the cinema of your mind as words, pictures, or a movie, allowing you to see the end before the beginning.

VISION — is a picture of something in your heart that is destined to be, that currently is not.

VISION — is the finished product produced in the unseen world, before manifesting itself in the seen world.

VISION — is a tangible and awesome picture of an opportunity for you to fulfil.

VISION — is the key to the door of opportunity that has been knocking at your heart.

VISION — is the key that opens the door to your destiny.

VISION — is what you see when opportunity knocks at the door.

VISION — says! "Behold I stand at the door and knock, if you will open the door I will come to you."

VISION — is a very clear picture of your future, your purpose and your destiny.

VISION — opens the door when opportunity knocks.

VISION — is what you see when your destiny comes knocking at the door of your heart.

VISION — is found under "V" in the filing cabinet of your heart, in there is filed the destiny for your entire life and faith is the key to the filing cabinet.

VISION — is what dreams are made of.

VISION — when followed by decision, will bring the provision and bring your life's mission to fruition.

VISION — will stop you from rolling with the punches and help you to start throwing them instead.

VISION — doesn't feel like a hunch it feels more like a punch.

VISION — the link between a vision and its fulfilment is your plans and your goals.

VISION — does not come into your heart as a potted plant but as a seed, which when watered, nurtured and pruned will eventually produce a magnificent harvest, which is your life purpose and destiny.

VISION — can be likened to FAITH, because they are both the substance of things hoped for and the evidence of things not yet seen.

VISION — can also be likened to HOPE, because they are both an anticipated expectation that will come to pass.

VISION — has the same function as a system, they both have the ability and responsibility to deliver a pre determined outcome.

VISION — has the ability to see things that are invisible.

Finally visions and dreams are the language of the Holy Spirit and because we are created in God's image we are part and parcel of that same language, being visions and dreams.

> "¹³*In the last days, God says, I will pour out my Spirit on all people. Your sons and daughters will prophesy, your young men will see visions, your old men will dream dreams.*"
> Acts 2:17

This verse does not mean that old men are not allowed to see visions and young men are not allowed to dream, dreams. The point here is that both are the language of the Holy Spirit and this is what God did when He created the Heavens and the earth, He saw it, (vision) He spoke it, it happened and then He liked what He saw as outlined in the example I have included here from the book of Genesis. (Have a look for yourself later in Genesis and you will see that when He created man He saw that it was <u>very</u> good)

> "⁹*And God said, 'Let the water under the sky be gathered to one place, and let dry ground appear.' And it was so. ¹⁰God called the dry ground 'land,' and the gathered waters he called 'seas.' And God saw that it was good.*"
> Genesis 1:9-10

MAKING YOUR VISION REAL

Goals are the carefully planned steps that you need to take in order to reach your vision, however if your vision is also your life purpose then you will never actually reach the end of it.

A life purpose is the very essence of who you are, why you are here and what you are prepared to pour your life into.

Mother Theresa's vision was to care for and feed the hungry, she knew this purpose would never be completed but she still gave her life for it.

It was her vision, her purpose and her destiny while she was here on earth rather than her destination and now that she has gone to heaven many thousands of others have caught her vision and continue to do what she gave her life for.

Vision is more caught than taught and if you are a leader or aspire to be a leader your responsibility is to clearly articulate and cast the vision of your corporation or establishment to your people, just like a fisherman would cast his line.

When they have caught the vision they can then run with it, but if they do not catch it then one of two things may be the problem. They are simply not interested in serving you and your vision or you have not clearly articulated it with passion and purpose. If many have caught it and just a few have not, then maybe they are just not interested. Being armed with a vision, a dream and a goal is not enough, you must now write them down and keep reminding yourself that you are prepared to pay the price to achieve them.

The Bible gives a very clear explanation of what we need to do.

> "*^{2}Then the LORD replied: 'Write down the revelation (vision) and make it plain on tablets (on paper) so that a herald (you) may run with it. ^{3} For the revelation awaits an appointed time; it speaks of the end (the fulfilment of it) and will not prove false (your vision won't lie to you). Though it linger, wait for it; it will certainly come and will not delay.'"*

Habakkuk 2:2 (Emphasis has been added in brackets.)

Write your vision down and then plan and set your goals very carefully to achieve it and watch it come to pass.

This chapter has one major point, you must have a vision and if you don't then there is not much point to your life.

You will pay a price for success and you will also pay a price for failure, it is your decision which price you are going to pay. Success is going to take work, discipline, passion and commitment to get there, but so does anything worth having.

Make a decision right now, that you will never give up and that you will run this human race all the way to the finish line.

> *"You will maximise your potential when you are willing to give up at any moment, all that you are to receive all that you can become."*
> Vince Lombardi (Coach of the Greenbay Packers - Superbowl Champions)

GETTING TO YOUR DESTINATION

We laid a foundation in an earlier chapter about four laws and one of these was the "The Law Of Aerodynamics".

The principles and keys to your vision and goals being reached are the same principles that the pilot of an aircraft must apply each and every time they fly. There is a flight plan the pilot must follow in order to reach the desired destination and there is a flight plan that you must follow in order to reach your destination.

THE KEY TO LIFE

"The responsibility of a plan is to deliver a pre-determined outcome"

I want you to see the check list and preparation that a pilot has to go through each and every time they fly, whether it is for a one hour flight or a 24 hour flight.

Your check list and life plan will determine whether you reach your destination and if you don't have one then any direction will get you there.

Your life journey is much longer than a pilot will travel and could take 70 years to complete, so before you take off you need to be prepared for the journey.

A PILOT'S CHECKLIST FOR THE VELOCITY AIRCRAFT

When they arrive at the airport, the first thing they must do is to look at the overall condition of the aircraft. Check for any big parts missing, damage to the plane, and fluids leaking (oil, fuel, and brake fluid). With checklist in hand, they will start with the pre—flight as stated. The following checklist is the one that is used at the factory for checkouts. It is a very basic checklist and they find that the more they look outside during flight, the better they handle the aircraft. They like to keep it short and right to the point, but at the same time, do all checks necessary for a safe flight. This checklist has been made available by Nathan Rigaud CF11.

A QUICK STORY BY NATHAN RIGAUD CF11

"A student and I were out training in the XLRG. About 10 miles out from the airport I told the student to look out the window on his side and as he looked, I pulled the gear pump breaker. He did not see what I did and he continued to fly and enter the pattern. We were on downwind and I told him to do his downwind checks at this time. I said no more. He started with gas, fuel pump on, then gear down. As he selected gear down, he had a puzzled look on his face.

Instead of working through the problem of not seeing the correct lights, he proceeded to the next step of mixture rich and prop full forward. On base leg I asked him if he was sure everything was OK with the aircraft. He said everything felt OK. On final I asked him if he was 100% sure that everything was done and was he happy with the plane. He replied that he thought so. As we approached the end of the runway and he started to round out for landing, I took over the controls and did a go-around. He asked why, and I told him that he just made a gear up landing (the wheels were not down) and he had made a mess of the plane. I pointed out the breaker that I pulled 10 miles out."

END OF STORY

The moral of this story is that if you are not 100% sure of anything during flight, then you must question it. When you are performing the checklist at any stage, be sure you are finished with one thing before going on to the next item."

It doesn't matter if you did not fully understand the technical flight language used in the story because the message is very clear. On the journey to your desired destination if you are not 100% sure of anything do not ignore the warning signs, be prepared to question your activity and make the necessary changes so that you do not crash land.

A PILOT'S PRE—FLIGHT CHECK LIST

Cockpit

Mags Off
Master On
Pitch Trim Check
Speed Brake Up and Down
Warning Lamps Check
Fuel Check
Outside Lights
Master Off
Canard Bolts and Nuts
Under the Panel
Elevator Bolt and Nut On and Tight
Mixture Idle Cut Off
Stick Free and Correct
Rudder Pedal Area Clear and Free
Airworthiness,
Registration,
Flight Manual,
W&B

Canard and Nose

Elevator Hinges and Weights Secure
Elevator Free and Correct
Pitot Tube Clearstatic Ports Clear
Nose Wheel
Proper Inflation
Wheel Pants Secure
Proper Tension On Wheel

HOW TO GET A VISION AND THEN SEE IT TO FRUITION

Hatch Covers Secure

Right Fuselage and Wing

Fuel Caps
Visually Check Fuel Quantity
Check O-Ring Condition
Secure Cap
Vortilons Secure
Leading Edge Check
Vertical Fin Check
Ruddercheck Free and Correct
Return Spring Secure
Hinge Pins
Aileron Free and Correct
Hinge Pinsright Main
Fairings / Gear Legs Condition
Brake Padstire Inflation and Condition

Left Fuselage and Wing

Same as Right Fuselage and Wing

Aft Fuselage and Engine

Fuel Sump Drain Check
Oil Level / Secure Stick and Door
Cowling Condition and Screws
Exhaust Tubes Secure
Aft Cowl Opening Clear Of Debris
Inlet Ducts Clear of Debris
Alternator Belt Check

Propeller Check For Nicks, Cracks, Erosion
Engine Area, No Leaks

Engine Start (Cold)

Mixture Rich
Throttle Open 1/8 Inch
Master Switch On
Fuel Pump On for 1 Second
Mags On
Propeller Clear
Brakes On
Starter Engage 1000 Rpm
Oil Pressure Check

Engine Start (Hot)

Mixture Idle Cut Off
Mixture Rich as Engine Starts 1000 Rpm
Oil Pressure Check

Before Taxi

Seat Belts On
Radio Master On

Before Take Off

Controls Free and Correct
Trim For Takeoff
Circuit Breakers In

Engine Run Up

1800 Rpm
Magneto Check
Propeller Cycle
Engine Instruments in Green
Suction In Greenthrottle 1000 Rpm
Flight Instruments Set
Fuel Pump On
Mixture Rich
Prop Inspeed Brake Up (if)Doors Locked
Final Approach Clear

Take Off

Maximum Throttlerotate 65-70Kts
Climb 90Kts
Positive Rate of Climb
Gear Up

500 Feet

25 Inches / 2500 Rpm
Fuel Pump Off / Check Pressure

Cruise

Use Your Power Settings
Engine Gauges in the Green

Descent and Landing

Circuit Breakers Inseat Belts

Downwind Check (GUMP)

(G) Fuel Pump On
(U) Undercarriage Down, Locked with 2 Green (120Kts Max)
(M) Mixture Rich
(P) Propeller In

Final

Gear Down 2 Green

Clear of Runway

Fuel Pump Off
Speed Brake Up

Shut Down

Avionics Off
Mixture Idle Cut Off
Mags Off
Lights Off
Master Off
Secure Aircraft

EMERGENCY PROCEDURES

Loss of Engine Power

Fly The Aircraft
Best Glide 100Kts
Mixture Rich
Mags On

Check Fuel Shutoff

Emergency Landing
121.50 Radio, 7700 Transponder
Master Off Before Touchdown
Mags Off
Fuel Shutoff In The Off Position
Fly the Aircraft to Landing

Engine Fire
Mixture Idle Cut Off
Magsfuel Shutoff In The Off Position
Land As Soon as Possible

In-flight Door Opening
Fly The Aircraft
Land as Soon as Possible

Wheel Brake Failure
Use The Longest Runway
Land Into the Wind if Possible
Use the Brake only if Necessary
Maintain Directional Control With Rudder and Good Brake

If the pilot follows the correct procedures it will allow him to land the aircraft within metres of his target every time, even after flying for 24 hours and 12,000 miles. Much of the flight would have been in darkness and possibly through violent storms, but the aircraft will still land according to the flight plan. On the way to your destination there may be hours of darkness, many storms and other circumstances that will cause you to have no visibility at all, but if you have prepared well and operate within the boundaries of your flight plan you will also land within metres of your target.

PUTTING IT ALL TOGETHER

We have already said that your vision will show you the end product in the unseen world before you have even started to build it in the seen world.

It is like seeing the completed picture of a jig saw puzzle on the outside of the box, yet when you open it there is 2,000 pieces that you have to put together.

You were prepared to pay the price to buy the jigsaw puzzle based on the picture you saw on the outside of the box but are you now prepared to pay the price to assemble it. It will come together one piece at a time, so before you start, make a decision to pay the price to finish it and design a plan of how you will assemble it.

Do you start with just any piece or do you put all the corner pieces in first and then the straight back pieces, so you will have an outline of the finished puzzle before you start with the middle of it. It is very important to keep the picture of the finished product very clearly in front of you at all times so that you can monitor your progress because some pieces look like they fit but that does not mean that they are right pieces.

The vision or the completed picture in your heart and mind works like a magnet and will draw you to it, now back to our pilot. I want you to parallel what we are doing with our pilot and apply it to

HOW TO GET A VISION AND THEN SEE IT TO FRUITION

your vision, your dreams, your goals and your destination. He is sitting in the Captain's seat of a 747 Jumbo Jet awaiting instructions from that small voice that talks to him through his head phones to take off on his 14-hour flight from Sydney to Honolulu.

His flight plan has been checked and entered into the aircraft's computer and he has his note pad with other instructions right next him. All the pre-flight checks have now been done and he has just received instructions to take off. He looks through the windscreen of the aircraft to make sure he has no obstacles in his path and that he has a very clear view of where he is going. The engine roars as he pushes the throttle all the way forward to create the speed and the momentum needed to get this giant aircraft off the ground. As the aircraft speeds down the runway the pre-take off procedures have not yet been completed, in a giant aircraft like this there are further safety procedures that must be followed.

At a certain speed down the runway the other pilot in the cockpit who is not actually doing the flying will call out V1 (Velocity One). This take off procedure is a very critical time in the aircraft's journey and is exactly the same principle you must apply when taking off on your journey. The co-pilot calls out V1 as a signal to the pilot that he is at the point of no return and there is now no going back, the aircraft must take off no matter what!

Many people get a vision, develop a flight plan, sit on the runway of their vision, push the throttle forward, but never get to V1 and therefore abort their take off. Anytime before V1 the aircraft can abort the take off and stop safely before the end of the runway and so can you but don't say things like, 'I can't do this thing so I will pull out while I still can', or 'I don't want to look stupid', or 'should I or should I not', or 'what if I really haven't got the talent or the commitment to make it happen', or 'what if my friends and family were right', or 'what if I can't find the money to complete it', or 'what if I fail', or 'when I do fail everyone will laugh at me', or they tell me 'I told you it wouldn't work' and so you justify why your vision never gets off the ground.

When you have your flight plan right and have checked all the conditions for your take off, do not just sit there and procrastinate. The Bible says that a "double minded person is unstable in all their ways", so when you make no decision, that is a decision, it is a decision to make no decision, (are you confused yet) which leads to confusion, double mindedness and will ultimately destroy your vision.

I am sure every time a pilot gets close to V1 on the runway of their journey they have some element of uncertainty and fear, but they know the only way to overcome that fear and uncertainty is to step into it with confidence and boldness. Boldness is not without fear or uncertainty, but it is overcoming fear and uncertainty by, doing it now!

When you get to V1 there is now no room for uncertainty because you are at the point of no return and if you try to abort now, just like the aircraft you will crash land, destroying all that you have worked for, so just do it, take off, obey the law of aerodynamics and fly like an eagle.

Now remember the law of gravity will always be trying to pull you back to earth where it would say you belong and the law of gravity may have many faces. Like your friends, your family, your peers and so on but just keep focussed on your vision and you will arrive.

YOUR VISION CHECKLIST

Here is a checklist based on the Law of Aerodynamics to use in fulfilling your vision and your destiny, as you are reading this checklist refer back to the Law of Aerodynamics in Chapter 2 if you need to refresh your understanding.

- I have counted the cost and understand that I will pay the price for success or I will pay the price for failure and I am committed to pay the price for success.

- My vision and my destination are very clear.

- My Flight Plan and goals are written, realistic and achievable.

- I carry them with me at all times, so that I can keep reading them to myself as a reminder of where I am going and how I am going to get there.

- I am prepared to change direction if necessary but will always seek the wisdom of the small voice that speaks to me when I pray and ask Him for advice.

- I will also seek advice from wise people I trust, because of the Biblical principle. "There is wisdom in a multitude of counsellors."

- My Vision Flight Plan is loaded into my Vision Flight Management System, which is my heart.

- I am the one sitting in the Pilot's seat and will take all responsibility for my vision to come to fruition.

- If I have a people coming on the journey with me, I am committed to them and realise that they will only reach their destination if I reach mine.

- I will not just let anyone come on my journey with me because I know there are many vision hijackers out there.

- I am prepared for a long journey and not just a short hop.

- I have got enough fuel to take off.

- I will stop for refuelling on the way and also take a breather.

- If it was good enough for God to only work 6 days then rest on the 7th day, when He created His vision (the heavens and the earth) then I will also take at least one day off each week.

- I know that just like an aircraft the hardest I will work is at the beginning and I am prepared for that.

- I will abort the take off if something goes wrong at V1, but I will not procrastinate if everything is clear for take off.

- Once I have reached V1 and everything is fine, I am committed to take off.

- I know I will encounter many dark nights and violent storms on the way to my destination because they are just part of life, but I will not stop until I have reached my destination.

- I will trust my flight plan and my built in horizon because they allow me to see even when storms, darkness and the whole of hell is unleashed against my vision.

- I know that the law of gravity is always lurking around and try-

HOW TO GET A VISION AND THEN SEE IT TO FRUITION

ing to pull me back to earth, but I will continue to obey the higher Law of Aerodynamics.

- If I happen to crash I will overcome the problems that caused it to happen and then I will get up and have another go.

- Irrespective of my current circumstances I make a promise to myself today that I will live the rest of my life as a winner, with a vision that I will bring to fruition.

Signed: _____

Today's Date: /   /

PART THREE – DIE A WINNER

CHAPTER SEVEN
ENOUGH OF THE MONKEY BUSINESS

Believe with me, that you were created on purpose, for a purpose by a God who not only has a plan for you in this life, but He is so loving that He has created a key that will open the door for you to live in Heaven with Him for eternity when you die. A Heaven where there is no more pain or suffering, but incredible joy and peace, this sounds too good to be true doesn't it? One of the reasons why people find this too hard to believe, is that they don't think they deserve such an awesome outcome after all the things they have done or have thought of doing in this life.

If it were true though, what a tremendous future and destiny you would have, because the bottom line would be, if you woke up in the morning on earth you win and if you died and woke up in Heaven you win.

ENOUGH OF THE MONKEY BUSINESS

If we did come from the big bang and our ancestors were monkeys and then before that they were a piece of green slime that crawled out of an ocean somewhere, we all have absolutely no hope or future.

The essence of evolution suggests that hydrogen, which is an odourless, colourless gas given enough time will turn into a person, but then so would a fish.

How can anything that just happened by some twist of fate or accident have any self worth, dignity, hope or future. Wouldn't it be quite a shock to you if you were the next person in line to experience an evolutionary change and as you were walking down the street, all of a sudden a little wing sprouted from your back? You have just become the first draft of the flying human beings, now don't laugh, because that is exactly what would have to happen if you were to believe in the ridiculous theory of evolution.

How does evolution give you any hope of a future when we get our self-worth from a sense of belonging and if we don't belong to anything then we have no value, no purpose and therefore no hope?

Millions of people are killing themselves because they have no sense of belonging, no self-image and no hope.

Imagine sitting down as most people do and showing your friends a photo album of your family, your parents, grand parents, great grand parents, great, great grandparents and lets imagine that you actually had photos of your family tree right back to the beginning of time. (That is from an evolutionists point of view.)

I can just see you now, showing everyone how very proud you are of your family heritage and I imagine that your conversation might go something like this. "See that monkey picking it's nose there in that photo, well he is from my Mother's side of the family, can't you see the incredible resemblance, (maybe some of you can, no I was only serious) maybe that is why I am always picking my nose and scratching my... "Now see these pieces of slime crawling out of the ocean in this photo, well they are what my Father's side of the family looked like before this photo here, where they had just days before and finally after millions of years turned into Kangaroos. That is obviously why my Dad won the Gold Medal at the Olympic Games for the High Jump and also obviously why we live in Australia."

Following is just a small portion of what is to come on the following pages, but because it is very relevant here I slotted it in from the greatest evolutionist of them all, Charles Darwin and Professor Conklin

CHARLES DARWIN, MY LIFE AND LETTERS VOL, 1, PAGE 210:

Admits. "Not one change of species into another is on record. We cannot prove that one single species has changed."

PROFESSOR EDWARD CONKLIN, READER'S DIGEST:

"The probability of life beginning from accident is comparable to the unabridged dictionary resulting from an explosion in a printing factory."

Mr Darwin and Professor Conklin pretty much smashed the whole theory of evolution right there, but there are many, many more admissions to come. If you sense some anger in my writing style as I tackle this subject you are right and I ask you to please hang in there with me because I am devastated about what this rubbish has done to the eternal prospects of multitudes of precious people. I want to expose it for the blatant lie that it is and deal it a mighty death blow so that everyone who has ever believed in evolution is set free.

I have great faith but I am sorry not enough faith to believe that rubbish and anyone who really believes that their family originated from a piece of green slime that was seen crawling out of an ocean, then became half a fish and half a donkey, then a giraffe or some other monstrosity has been aptly described by a world authority, Doctor James Gray.

He says the following about anyone who could possibly believe in evolution in one of his articles. "It would be a figment of a deranged brain." You will read his full article in the next few pages.

A couple of days ago on television a man who was facing trial for murder was freed after the fifth time that he had been on trial for this same crime. The news reader said that one of the reasons why he was freed was because of the testimony of a key witness in the trial. This person apparently lost credibility when they told the court that they were the reincarnation of a famous race horse. For the life of me I cannot understand why anyone would lose their credibility for thinking that they were a race horse, can you?

If you believe in evolution then you might as well believe in reincarnation and if you were on the jury you could have convinced the court that this person was a famous race horse and that their admission should not affect their credibility.

"If that person is reading this book let me assure you I am not making fun of you but you are not a famous race horse, but you do have one thing in common with him and that is, you were also born a winner, can live a winner, but unlike him you can also die a winner."

Why don't you all try going to your local zoo and telling the zoo keeper that you are related to Tony the male chimpanzee and that you want to take him home to meet the rest of the family for a couple of days, they will have you locked up.

Millions of precious people throughout the centuries have been sold this blatant lie of evolution and it is one of the greatest crimes against humanity ever committed. If you currently believe this theory stay with me because you have been led to read this book so that I can show you that you are an awesome, special, one of a kind, created on purpose for a purpose child of the living God and have an incredible destiny in front of you.

If I had several sugar cubes in my hand, do you think anyone would object to me crushing them and throwing them in the rubbish? It may be said that I am a bit wasteful, but I am sure most people would not even care. On the other hand what would happen if I was having a cup of coffee in a shopping centre and got up and killed the three people sitting at the next table and then threw them into the rubbish? I would be arrested, convicted of murder and depending on which country I was in, either given life in prison or sentenced to death.

The sugar cube that was created on purpose, for a purpose can be destroyed without even raising an eyebrow and yet the human beings who supposedly have no creator and only came into existence by some strange accident or big bang, without any preplanned purpose at all are not allowed to receive the same treatment. I think maybe right now I need some help, because this makes no sense to me at all. If the evolution theory is right, then we have no value, no hope and no future, so why should we not be able to treat human beings just the same as the sugar cubes?

The lie that we have no real purpose and therefore no real value, abides in the mind of millions of people rich and poor across the face of our planet. I have indicated already that this book is being written to set people free, by exposing this and many other blatant lies that have bound people up and made them slaves to hopelessness and fear.

The sugar cube was designed and created by the hand of man, but you my special friend were designed and created by the hand of God, the creator of the entire Universe and all that is in it.

WHAT THE EXPERTS HAVE ADMITTED ABOUT EVOLUTION:

Here is what some of the world's most acclaimed evolutionists, naturalists, anthropologists, biologists and other world authorities have said and admitted to about evolution versus creation. These extracts are personal quotes from these world authorities dating back to about 1860.

PROFESSOR LEJEUNE

Said his chromosomal research had shown that "Genetic differences between man and apes were so great that the human species could not have evolved from some primeval chimpanzee or gorilla," THE ADVERTISER, ADELAIDE, FEBRUARY 18, 1978.

CHARLES DARWIN

Asks: "Why, if species descended from other species by fine graduations, do we not find everywhere innumerable transitionary forms?"

What would Mr Darwin say today when research has defined 3,000,000 species with not a single connecting link.

PROFESSOR EINSTEIN

"The World As I See It" wrote, "The scientist's religious feeling takes the form of rapturous amazement, at the perfect harmony of natural law, which reveals intelligence of such superiority that compared with it, all systemic thinking and acting of human beings is an utterly insignificant reflection."

PROFESSOR JAMES GRAY

In his Presidential address to Section D. (Zoology) of the British Association, asks, "Why should we accept the spontaneous origin of life? If considered as an observable phenomenon, if any other sphere of human thought, it would be discarded as a figment of a deranged brain. Is there any evidence of a dynamic (extremely complicated) machine coming into existence (spontaneously)? The belief in the spontaneous origin of life is a negation of the very principles of science."

LOREN C. EISLEY, ANTHROPOLOGIST

"Scientific American, flatly states, "Ants have changed very little if at all. They are one of the small immortals."

In Harper's Magazine, November, 1955, in an article entitled, "Was Darwin right about the human brain?" wherein he discusses this question with Dr Alfred Russell Wallace these facts emerge, "Man's brain from his creation has the same potential as now. Man's brain capacity has not increased. Men of the Mesopotamian valley of 5,000 years ago were as intelligent as our generation, although they did not have the accumulation of knowledge to draw upon."

He further writes: "Man and his rise now appear short in time. Explosively short! Whatever the forces involved in the production of the human brain, a long, slow competition of human groups would not result in such similar mental potentialities among all people everywhere. Something or some other factor has escaped our scientific attention."

Something has escaped their attention, God created man in His image and God would hardly look like a piece of green slime.

MAURICE MAETERLINCK, NATURALIST

"The Life Of The Ant" Writes; Ants are the most abundant in fossil of any animal, eleven thousand specimens have been examined and in spite of millions of years, contrary to expectation and a most disconcerting fact to the evolutionist. The most ancient are as we find them today, and thus were, as the Bible states, "Created."

Since the atomic age has been ushered in we have come to understand that matter is not eternal. It is pent—up energy. It had a beginning and may be destroyed. In his book, "Why we believe in creation and not evolution", page 273, Meldau quotes Sir Ambrose Fleming as saying, "Between space, and space filled with even the most rarefied matter, there is a gulf which no theory of evolution has been able to pass or explain."

Meldau goes on to say, "Nothing cannot produce matter, (Atoms) Genesis 1:1 and Hebrews 11:3 give the only answer. Between matter and motion there is a similar gulf. There is no greater attested fact of science, than the fact that it takes power to put inert matter into motion. No evolutionary theory we have ever heard of attempts to explain the origin of both matter and motion unless it concedes a prime cause – God. Life cannot come into being except from previous life."

Hence the universal law, you cannot have creation without a creator, there is no argument and that is the end of it!

IRWIN SCHROEDINGER, NOBLE LAUREATE IN PHYSICS

Was quoted in an article. "The Greatest Mystery Of All The Secrets Of Life." by Waldemar Kaempffert, as saying. "Where are we when presented with the mystery of life? We find ourselves facing a granite wall which we have not even chipped; we know virtually nothing of growth, nothing of life."

DOCTOR AUSTIN H. CLARK, BIOLOGIST SMITHSONIAN INSTITUTE, WASHINGTON:

Said, "There are no such things as missing links. Missing links are misinterpretation." Noack, page 22.

In "Did man just happen?" Criswell, page 60, quotes Professor Vircow who once wrote, "The ape—man has no existence and the missing links are a phantom."

CHARLES DARWIN

"The absence of transitional forms between the species presses hard on my theory."

Again, "Geology assuredly does not reveal any such finely graded organic chain; this is the most obvious and gravest objection urged against my theory." Origin of Species, Vol 2, Chapter 9, 6th Edition.

What does he mean "presses hard against my theory, or the most obvious and gravest objection," this is what he is really saying!

My entire life's work has been trying to prove there is no God, but it has amounted to absolutely nothing, all I have done is prove more and more that there is a God.

Mr. Darwin influenced millions of people to agree that there is no God and now they like him, are probably lost for eternity and that is very, very sad.

Imagine the impact Charles Darwin would have had, if only he gave his life to proving that there is a God and that He loves us beyond our wildest understanding.

DOUGLAS DEWAR, BRITISH NATURALIST

Once an ardent evolutionist says: "Palaeontology (study of fossils) cannot be regarded other than a hostile witness against evolution, the earliest known fossils of each class and order are not half developed, but have all the essential characteristics of their class or order."

In the book "Is Evolution Proved"? Dewar quoted J. William

Dawson, F.R.S (Geologist), McGill University, Montreal, who once said, "The evolutionist doctrine is itself one of the strangest phenomena of humanity. That, in our day, a system destitute of even a shadow of proof, should be accepted as a philosophy, and this, in spite of our vast and weighty stores of knowledge, is surpassing strange."

DOCTOR HERBERT NILSSON, PROFESSOR OF BOTANY, UNIVERSITY OF LUND, SWEDEN

After a life study of genetics and fossil records says, "As we look at the main groups of fossil flora, we find that at definite intervals they are, all at once and quite suddenly, there! In full bloom in all their manifold forms, any change is entirely lacking.

He concludes, "All my investigations have led to incredible contradictions, on account of which the theory of evolution ought to be entirely abandoned. It is a serious obstruction to biological research."

And again, "My attempts to demonstrate evolution by experiments carried out for over 40 years, have completely failed. The final results of my investigations and studies, always leads to incredible contradictions." (Selections from Synthetische, Artildung, 1954.)

DOCTOR AUSTIN H. CLARK, F.R.G.S., NOTED BIOLOGIST OF SMITHSONIAN INSTITUTE

Says, "While man's body structure is most like that of man—like apes, all the early remains of pre—historic man are distinctly those of man.

No animals are known even from the earliest rocks, which cannot at once be assigned to their proper phylum or major group. If we accept the facts, the major groups from the first, bore the same relationship to each other as they do at present." Meldau, page 316.

CHARLES DARWIN, MY LIFE AND LETTERS VOL, 1, PAGE 210

Admits. "Not one change of species into another is on record. We cannot prove that one single species has changed."

DOCTOR. PAUL FRANCIS KERR, NOTED MINERALOGIST:

Says. "I cannot believe that the facts of science are mere accidents.

What I have studied about the earth, has increased my belief in a Supreme Power, God must be. "Only an infallible mind could have adjusted our world and its life, in its amazing intricacies." Meldau, Page 50

SCIENTIFIC AMERICAN, JULY, 1954

"Our earth turns on its axis once every 24 hours. Once a year we spin around the sun in an orbit of almost 600 million miles. The amazing accuracy, with which the universe revolves as a perfect and flawless machine, can be seen in the perfection of our journey around the sun.

It takes the earth 365 days, 5 hours, 48 minutes and 48 seconds; it has not varied one second in 1,000 years."

THE KEY TO LIFE

REAR ADMIRAL D.V. GALLERY, U.S.N. SATURDAY EVENING POST

Wrote, "The stars in their orbits and velocities through the heavens faithfully obey a great code of law. Earth's scientists can quote and explain this code in great detail, until you ask. Whence came these laws"?

When we look at the marvels of this universe we can only but agree with the writer who said. "It were as easy to believe that Milton's Paradise were set up in all it's stately march of balanced syllables by an ape, or that the letters of balanced syllables by an ape, or that the letters composing it had been blown together by a whirlwind, as to believe that the visible universe about us, built upon mathematical laws, knitted together by a million correspondences, and crowned thick with marks of purpose, is the work of a mindless force." Dr Fitchett.

PROFESSOR L. VICTOR CLEVELAND

Commenting on the inability of science to produce life in the test tube, in his anti—evolution compendium, says, "So far as all the scientists can prove, there is no such thing as spontaneous generation, life must come from antecedent life." And, "Not a bacterium, nor algae, nor salpa worm, nor anything else ever evolved higher. Check the facts and see." (What about green slime? - sorry, I could'nt help myself!)

THE LIVING SEA

"Most of the 12,000 kinds of fossil insects identified are similar to living species." Even Huxley, the hard boiled evolutionist admits.

"The only difference between the fossil and the animal of today is that one is older than the other."

H. GRACEY, EVOLUTION AND THE HONEY BEE

Says, "In this little insect, we have a trap to catch and baffle the ablest men that ever tried to support the evolutionary theory. In the Honey Bee we have a highly endowed little creature with instincts that seem to rival reasoning powers more closely than the instincts of any other creature and yet, there is no door left open for the entrance or the transmission of these wonderful peculiarities. The parents of the bee, the Queen and the Drone, have none of these instincts to transmit. The Honey Bee itself, which has no offspring, can transmit nothing."

Darwin's theory is closed both ends and this is the hand of God. "The evolution theory demands a world teeming with intermediate forms of life" Darwin. Which all must acknowledge would mean teeming hopeless monstrosities with half developed limbs, wings, bones, feathers, fins, need I add more? Yet all, even the most stubborn evolutionist will admit that the record of bones and fossil reveals not a single example. (there goes your photo album)

CHARLES DARWIN

Said, "I imagine that probably all organic beings which ever lived on earth, descended from some primitive form which was first called into life by the Creator." After Its Kind, Nelson, Page 15.

Many evolutionists now believe and teach this and it is also being taught in many universities, but while it is a big concession it must be rejected as it is directly opposed to the Genesis record, which is emphatic that all life was created, in fixed species (**same species**), to bring forth after their own kind as it says in, GENESIS CHAPTER ONE.

BYRON C. NELSON, TM.M., "AFTER IT'S KIND," 1961

"Genesis 1:24 reads. "God said; let the earth bring forth the living creatures after their kind." After its kind, repeated six times in Genesis 1 is a statement of a biological principle that no human observation has ever known to fail."

THOMAS HUXLEY, FAMOUS EVOLUTIONIST "CRITIQUES AND ADDRESSES," PAGE 182:

Admits, "If we confine ourselves to positively ascertained facts, in the animal and vegetable kingdom, there has been little apparent change from their first appearance to the present time."

PROFESSOR JAMES PARK

Textbook of Geology, page 265, "The obvious lesson from the study of fossils is the elementary truth that life even in the earliest times, differed in no way from life today."

"Further, we observe that the lower types of life that appear in the oldest rocks have persisted through all geological times, up to the present day."

PROFESSOR CAULTERY OF THE CHAIR OF EVOLUTION, UNIVERSITY OF PARIS, "SCIENCE 1938"

"The general fact, that palaeontology shows us few transitional forms, and still, fewer primitive forms is very disturbing."

The "few forms", of course, are fragments which even they disagree on.

PROFESSOR COULTER, SCHOOL SCIENCE SERIES, PAGE 16

"Darwin's explanation of organic evolution is now an inadequate explanation."

Fifty years ago the following authorities said.

DOCTOR SCOTT

Nature, "A generation has grown up that knows not Darwin."

JOHN BURROUGHS

Atlantic Monthly, "Darwin has been shorn of his selection theories, as completely as Samson was shorn of his locks."

PROFESSOR BATESON

Nature, Darwin speaks no more than with philosophical authority."

PROFESSOR HOLMES

Science, "The present theory of evolution is bankrupt."

BYRON C. NELSON "AFTER IT'S KIND", PAGES 103-106

Refers to Mendel's Law of heredity, or Principles of Genetics, now almost universally accepted, which has completely changed the old ideas of scientists in regard to heredity and evolution generally. He quotes the following: "Biologist, Biologist, "Darwin would never have written "ORIGIN OF SPECIES" had he known Mendel's Law, which also has gone far to destroy the faith of biologists in evolution itself." This was stressed by PROFESSOR CAULLERY of the CHAIR OF EVOLUTION OF PARIS at HARVARD UNIVERSITY.

E.W. MCBRIDE, PROFESSOR of ZOOLOGY, IMPERIAL COLLEGE OF SCIENCES, ENGLAND:

Says in effect, "It has led evolutionists into a blind alley."

Acquired Characters are a basic principle of the evolution theory; today it is universally rejected by scientists."

PROFESSOR LOCK, VARIATION, HEREDITY, AND EVOLUTION, PAGE 115:

Says of evolutionists, "It is generally agreed among them that acquired characters are not inherited."

PROFESSOR KELLOG, EVOLUTION THE WAY OF MAN, PAGE 97:

Writes, "Unfortunately it does not seem to happen."

PROFESSOR CONKLIN, HEREDITY AND ENVIRONMENT PAGE 240

Says, "The inheritance of acquired characters is inconceivable."

PROFESSOR EDWARD CONKLIN, READER'S DIGEST

"The probability of life beginning from an accident, is comparable to the unabridged dictionary resulting from an explosion in a printing factory."

MR. ETHERIDGE, PALAEONTOLOGIST, BRITISH MUSEUM

Once said, "There is not one iota of proof in this great Museum for the transmutation of species." Quoted in "DID MAN JUST HAPPEN?"

PAGE 18. LECOMTE DU NOUY, HUMAN DESTINY

Admitted, "Each group, order, or family seems to be born suddenly, when we discover them, they are already differentiated." Of birds, he says. "They have all the unsatisfactory characteristics of absolute creation."

SIR ARTHUR KEITH

Said, "Evolution is unproven and unprovable. We believe it because the only alternative is special creation." Professor D.M. Watson, London University, said, in effect, that this holds for evolutionists generally, quoted page 46, "DID MAN JUST HAPPEN?"

Again Criswell quotes Professor Branco, who says, "Man appeared suddenly in the Quaternary period. Palaeontology tells us nothing on the subject. It knows no ancestors of man," page 60.

ERIC WASSMAN, MODERN BIOLOGY AND THEORY OF EVOLUTION

Writes. "The whole hypothetical pedigree of man is not supported by a single fossil genus of a single fossil species."

PROFESSOR WILLIAM L. STRAUSS. JR., QUARTERLY REVIEW OF BIOLOGY

"Missing links are as conspicuous by their absence as they were one hundred years ago."

PROFESSOR RENDLE SHORT

Said, "The further back we look for early man the more like us he appears to be." Quoted page 61, "DID MAN JUST HAPPEN?"

AFRICAN SKULLS

Some years ago a great stir was made over remains found in South Africa, claimed to be an ape man, together with tools. Like most such finds, the reports were most misleading. It is now agreed that the tools had no connection with the bones which were found in a cave, while the tools were from a river bed and it is generally agreed that all the bones were those of apes.

W.A. CRISSWELL

Writes also, page 73, "Doctor Rudolph Virchow of Berlin University, once pleaded with his fellow scientists not to teach the theory of evolution as fact. "Because it is insupportable and not capable of demonstration."

At the Munich Congress, Virchow said in part, "If generatio aequivoca, (spontaneous generation), were capable of proof it would indeed be beautiful! But the proofs of it are still wanting. Those familiar with the failure to find support for the theory," he adds, "will feel it doubly serious to demand that this discredited theory should be in any way accepted as the basis of all our views of life."

Quoted from "The old riddle and the newest answer," John Gerard, Page 24.

J.R. HAND

"Why I accept the Genesis record," page 27, PROFESSOR T.H. MORGAN, CALIFORNIAN INSTITUTE, OF TECHNOLOGY says,

"Within the period of human history we do not find a single instance of the transmutation of one species into another one."

PROFESSOR E.A. HOOTON, HARVARD UNIVERSITY

Said, "The alleged restorations of ancient types of men have little, if any, scientific value," quoted page 38 in, "WHY I ACCEPT THE GENESIS RECORD", BY J.R. Hand.

The same author, page 46, "SIR ARTHUR KEITH, ROYAL COLLEGE OF SURGEONS, FORMER PRESIDENT OF THE ROYAL ANTHROPOLOGICAL INSTITUTE, has said, "Embryology provides no support for the evolution hypothesis."

DOCTOR McNAIR WILSON, EDITOR OXFORD MEDICAL PUBLICATIONS

"Increase of knowledge about biology has tended to emphasise the extreme rigidity of type, and more and more, to discount the idea of transmutation from one type to another, the essential basis of Darwinism. The classis aphorism, (when a mule breeds), ought to serve as a warning against the easy acceptance of a theory which is as full of ogres, mermaids, and centaurs as any fairy tale," page 49.

PROFESSOR H.H. NEWMAN, CHICAGO UNIVERSITY

Said, "reluctant as he may be to admit it, honesty compels the evolutionist to admit that there is no absolute proof of organic evolution", page 56 of "WHY I ACCEPT THE GENESIS RECORD", J. R. Hand.

And the same booklet on page 66, he quotes two authorities, PROFESSOR WILLIAM J. TINKLE, LA VERNE COLLEGE. The first says, "The most ancient man known to us is not essentially different from the man now living", and the second, "Cro-Magnon man averaged 6 feet in height and had a cranial capacity 150cc above that of modern man and, living at the same time were Neanderthal men with a cranial (brain) capacity equal to that of modern man." How could one be descended from the other?"

DOCTOR THOMAS DWIGHT, THOUGHTS OF A CATHOLIC ANATOMIST, PAGE 20

Says, "The tyranny in the matter of evolution, (in scientific circles), is overwhelming, to a degree of which the outsider has no idea." Many scientists have voiced the same thing.

SIR EDWARD POULTON, F.R.S., ESSAYS ON EVOLUTION, PAGE 193

"Although no one strove so nobly against such odds in its defence, Huxley was at no time a convinced believer in the theory which he protected."

SIR ISAAC NEWTON

Almost three hundred years ago in "Principia" 2nd edition, recorded. "The most beautiful system of the sun, planets and comets, could only proceed from the counsel and dominion of an intelligent and powerful Being."

CHARLES DARWIN, ORIGIN OF SPECIES, 6TH EDITION, PAGE 286

Admits. "If my theory be true, vast periods must have swarmed with living creatures before the Cambrian period."

Darwin's day saw no evidence of these "vast swarms" and he later admits, "The difficulty of assigning any good reason for the absence of vast piles of strata, rich in fossils beneath the Cambrian system is very great, the case at present must remain inexplicable and may be truly used as a valid argument against the views here entertained."

In the "EVOLUTION OF PLANTS" page 37; referring to the sudden unexplainable appearance of flowering plants, together with pollinating insects, wasps and bees, he calls it an "abominable mystery."

PROFESSOR W. B. SCOTT, AN INTRODUCTION TO GEOLOGY, PAGE 288, 3RD EDITION, VOLUME 2

Says of the sudden appearance of the flora, "With extreme suddenness the invasion swept the earth. There can be no question as to the facts of the completeness of the revolution of the flora."

Interesting how he said "with extreme suddenness the invasion swept the earth." This sudden invasion fits with the Bible account of God saying in Genesis, "Let it be and it was." (That's pretty sudden isn't it!)

PROFESSOR R. VIRCHOW

Writes in "THE NEW MATERIALISM, page 83, "There has been a beginning of life, since geology points to epochs in the formation of the earth when life was impossible."

F.W. NOACK, THE THEORY OF EVOLUTION IN THE LIGHT OF SCRIPTURE AND NATURE, PAGE 30

Quotes Professor Fleischman of Eriangen, Zoologist, as saying, "The Darwinian theory of descent has not a single fact to confirm it in the realm of nature, it is purely the product of the imagination."

SIR CHARLES BELL, UNIVERSITY COLLEGE, LONDON.

Has said, "Everything declares the species to have it's origin in distinct creation."

Let's finish off with this amazing bit of creative genius. If you want evolution here is real evolution. Lets have a look at the frog, first an egg, then a fish with a long tail, next two front legs, then two back legs, then off comes the tail, and out hops the frog onto the ground. Here, by the inherent law of the creator we see, in a few weeks what the evolutionist claims would require millions of years. The truth is that no link of an intermediate stage has ever been found. How unfortunate for the evolutionist that the platypus has survived. Had only fragments of this creature been found in fossil form it could well have been used to boost the evolution theory more than anything else has done. But, alas, he lives as a living contradiction to this ridiculous theory, God has a few tricks up His sleeve just to keep them honest.

The Bible says this!

> "[20]*For since the creation of the world God's invisible qualities—his eternal power and divine nature—have been clearly seen, being understood from what has been made, so that men are without excuse.*"
> Romans 1:20

CHAPTER EIGHT
THE PROOF OF THE PUDDING IS IN THE EATING

We have established that your physical birth was an awesome miracle and that you won your heat, which was that incredible race you had to win to be born. You are now running in the semi final and by the time you have finished reading this chapter, you will know how to qualify for and win the final.

It would have been easier for me to write this book about the fact that you were born a winner, to live a winner and leave the part out about you being able to die a winner.

This would have been enough for many of you to go out and experience awesome earthly success, but only in this life.

THE PROOF OF THE PUDDING IS IN THE EATING

Talking about life after death can be like talking about politics, most people do not want to go there and if someone does they are often told to shut up and then never invited to another party.

There is not just two parts to your life's story, there are three and I am not going to shut up so I can be accepted by the crowd and invited to the next party. There is a much more important party to be invited to and that's the one I am about to tell you about.

I am compelled to tell you all three parts of the story because your life depends on it, or I should say your eternal life depends on it and that to me is without doubt the most valid of all reasons to risk offending you.

To keep this incredible story of transformation that can take place in your life to myself, knowing that it will lead you to eternal life would be my crime against humanity.

Let's imagine for a moment that you are living next to a bridge that spans a river which lies 100 metres below. One night while you are lying warm and snug in your bed and listening to a torrential storm outside, you hear the bridge begin to break apart and crash into the river below. You know that this will leave an expanse of 500 metres between one side of the river and the other and you also know that any second, many motorists would be coming over the hill on their approach to the bridge, totally unaware of the danger which lay ahead.

Right now you hold THE KEY TO EARTHLY LIFE for these people in your hands and it is up to you as to whether they are going to reach their destination, so what are you going to do. Will you stay in bed where you are comfortable and warm or will you get up, grab a lamp and run out into the storm so you can save them from the jaws of death?

This story is no different perhaps than your current situation as it may reveal the expanse between where you are right now and where you need to be, so I am getting out of my warm and comfortable zone right now, grabbing my lamp and running out into the storm of your life, so that I can show you THE KEY TO LIFE which will save you from plunging into the jaws of death and to a lost eternity.

Twenty odd years ago a miraculous transformation took place in my life and has taken place in the lives of millions of other people just like you and me.

This is my story and so I promise to tell you the truth, the whole truth and nothing but the truth. We can argue with doctrine and theories until we are blue in the face but we cannot argue with real true life testimonies, because they happened and that is that.

The word selling in the dictionary means "to impart" and successful salespeople whether they are aware of it or not, know how to impart the benefits (or true testimony) of their product or service to the customer. And when they have done that successfully, The Price / Value Formula takes over.

THE PRICE / VALUE FORMULA

"When the perceived value of my product or service in the customer's mind, exceeds the price they will have to pay by one dollar, the customer will buy my product or service."

This formula is about changing people's perception and this book is about changing your perception of your existence, your life and your eternal destination. True testimony of something that has actually happened is the most powerful way to change anyone's perception and that is why Jesus said it in the Bible.

> "*[15] But in your hearts set apart Christ as Lord. Always be prepared to give an answer to everyone who asks you to give the reason for the hope that you have. (This is a testimony) But do this with gentleness and respect, [16] keeping a clear conscience, so that those who speak maliciously against your good behaviour in Christ may be ashamed of their slander."*
> 1Peter 3:15-16

Jesus was clearly instructing Christians to be ready at all times to share a testimony about what He has done for them and on that note let me make something very, very clear. Jesus never, ever said to bash anyone over the head with the Bible, or with judgement, or with condemnation and guilt.

If you have ever been mentally or physically mistreated, judged or condemned by anyone in the name of God, let me assure you that is not the God of Heaven, it is satan, and he uses man made religions to mislead people about God who loves you.

God has nothing to do with driving people and loves us so much that He let His own Son Jesus die on a cross for us and why would He do that if His intention was to hurt us? Here is something that you must never forget even if at this moment it is not quite clear to you. The Holy Spirit leads but satan drives, so if you are being driven in any way it is not from God, it is from satan.

The umpire of the presence and the will of God in your life is a peace that is beyond your natural understanding, a peace that reigns even when the whole of hell is being unleashed against you.

The Bible mentions the word "love" or associated words like loving, loved, loving kindness and the like over 450 times, so this should give you an idea about how much God loves you.

Here is just one scripture from the Bible which sums up His incredible love for you.

> "*16 For God so loved the world that he gave his one and only Son, that whoever believes in him shall not perish but have eternal life. 17 For God did not send his Son into the world to condemn the world, but to save the world through him.*"
> John 3:16-17

This chapter is called 'THE PROOF OF THE PUDDING IS IN THE EATING' and it is called that because I want to share two testimonies with you. One happened to Paul the Apostle around 2,000 years ago and the other which is mine happened around 2,000 years later, but both are remarkably similar.

I hope we have built a trusting relationship so far and that you will stick with me as I take you on this amazing journey that may challenge your entire belief system. It will encourage and bring you hope so keep your heart open, because you are about to learn how you too can win the final.

The Bible talks about a spiritual birth and it calls it being "Born Again."

THE PROOF OF THE PUDDING IS IN THE EATING

> *"³In reply Jesus declared, 'I tell you the truth, no one can see the kingdom of God unless he is born again.' ⁴'How can a man be born when he is old?' Nicodemus asked. 'Surely he cannot enter a second time into his mother's womb to be born!' ⁵Jesus answered, 'I tell you the truth, no one can enter the kingdom of God unless he is born of water and the Spirit. ⁶Flesh gives birth to flesh, but the Spirit gives birth to spirit. ⁷You should not be surprised at my saying, 'You must be born again.'"*
> John 3:3-7

When the Bible talks about man, it refers to mankind and that is men, women and children.

One night, in a little church, actually it was an old wooden community hall in a country town in Australia I experienced what the Bible says is to be "Born Again."

I had never read the Bible and had absolutely no idea about God, Jesus, the Holy Spirit or even what a Christian was.

I did know however that I was an alcoholic mess that may have looked alright on the outside because I was an exercise fanatic, but was an absolute mess on the inside.

Nothing ever satisfied me, even though I tried most things I could not fill the void that was in my heart. As the saying goes I tried sex, drugs and rock n' roll, but none of them could take away the emptiness I felt on the inside and because of this I would drink myself to sleep almost every night.

My life was full of grief, broken relationships, violence and loneliness even when I was the life of the party, which was most of the time. I had unfulfilled dreams, but could never seem to focus on them for long enough to bring them to pass.

I believed the very lie that I wrote about earlier, that when we die we are placed in a coffin, tossed into the ground, eaten by worms and then lost for all eternity. I thought if there was a God, He obviously didn't care about me or anyone else and so why should I care about me or anyone else.

I was an unstable man in an unstable relationship at the time and the thought of establishing a family with a wife and children that would be taken away from me at death, was too much for me to bear. So without being conscious of it at the time I would destroy every relationship that got too close, because I knew it would end up in pain.

I thought if there was a God then He must be some sort of sadist to set us up for devastation after He had promised so much by giving us life in the first place and therefore alcohol, sex, night clubs, training my body and all other forms of self gratification became my God.

My brother who is a Christian was visiting me in this little country town on a working holiday from New Zealand and one day he asked me if I would like to go with him to this little Church of about 50 people he was attending while he was staying with me called the Christian Outreach Centre. Because I was doing nothing that night except going to a hotel to get drunk again I accepted his invitation.

My only previous experience with Church showed me that it was a boring place, so dead and boring in fact that if someone died in a pew, the ambulance officers would have to go through 30 rows of people checking all of their pulses including the preacher to find the dead person.

This Church was certainly not like that as everybody was full of life and joy. There was a beautiful presence and peace that permeated the entire building which was something that I had never experienced before.

The Bible says that the Church is no longer just a building as it was before Jesus died and rose again, but Jesus said that He would come and live inside us and that the believers are the Church.

He obviously meant it because when I invited Him to come and live inside of me I have never been the same to this very day. When you have the creator of the entire universe living on the inside, you will not need your pulse checked to see if you are alive, because people will see the life of Jesus in your eyes.

The word "Enthusiasm" is used by almost every motivational speaker in the world and whether they realise it or not, the word literally means "God Within" and when God lives within, the whole of hell can be going on without, but you will have His strength and power to stand no matter what comes against you.

The power of God I experienced that night and countless times since was totally unexpected, but I made a decision to open my heart and put my trust in Him. I asked God if He was there to please reveal Himself to me and to make me whole.

After we all sat down the Pastor got up, welcomed everyone to the service and then the worship leader together with the band led the congregation in singing these beautiful songs about Jesus, the Holy Spirit and God.

As explained before I had no previous experience with Church, so I was completely ignorant of who God, Jesus and the Holy Spirit were, in fact I did not even know that they were related, but I joined in the singing anyway.

Within minutes of the worship starting my entire being was soaked inside and out with this incredible Heavenly presence. I felt like I was standing under a waterfall of thick golden love and glory which was pouring all over and through me.

It was so beautiful, magnificent and powerful that I had to fight to stay on my feet because all I really wanted to do was fall over, lie down and bath in this unbelievable presence.

All of a sudden I broke into convulsive tears, the kind of tears that a baby cries when they are out of control and need mummy or daddy to pick them up. As I stood there I could feel all of this rubbish and pain coming to the surface of my entire being, then just draining away.

It was the most incredible experience I have ever had and it felt like I was literally in the arms of Jesus, which I never wanted to stop.

My brother approached me and asked if I would like to walk to the front and have the Pastor pray for me to lead me in a prayer to accept Jesus Christ as my Lord and Saviour.

I had no idea what this meant but I knew, that I knew that it was the right thing to do. My heart was racing and all I wanted to do was to have Jesus hold me in His arms and set me free. I felt totally drunk on this presence and found it difficult to actually walk out the front, but it was a beautiful drunk feeling, not that out of control alcohol drunk feeling.

When I arrived at the altar, the Pastor walked up to me, smiled, then asked me if I would you like to accept Jesus as my Lord and Saviour and I said, YES!

He then very lightly placed his hand on my forehead and asked me to follow him in a prayer, which went something like this.

"Lord Jesus I come to you now and ask you to forgive me of my sins, I believe that you died on the cross for me and I accept you now as my Lord and my Saviour. I ask you to please come and live in my heart so that I will be Born Again and receive eternal life."

I was not aware at the time but there were four men including my brother standing behind me, for a reason that I was about to discover.

The very moment I had finished praying that prayer, what seemed like a bolt of love which was like lighting went through me (it was beautiful) and I was flat on my back in the arms of these four men who lowered me to the floor.

I weighed around 100kgs at the time and was a very aggressive and violent person, who prided himself at having never being put down in a fight, but God had other ideas and obviously for a good reason.

I was told later that I lay on the floor for around 45 minutes totally oblivious of what was going on in the Church and I never even heard the Pastor preaching.

THE KEY TO LIFE

The service had finished when I got up off the floor and the people were all standing around having a cup of tea. I now know that the floor is God's operating table, a place where He can keep us still for long enough to operate on our spirit, to take away our sin, our pain and impart to us His healing power, His strength and vision for our lives.

While I was on the floor I heard what I thought were Angels singing and harps playing this most awesome music. The voices were all worshipping God and during this time all the pain in my life continued to simply wash away.

When I finally got off the floor I felt as light as a feather, totally refreshed, full of joy and peace and all I wanted to do was hear all about Jesus. That night when I got home I started reading the Bible and whenever I read about or saw the name of Jesus I would just cry, then when the crying had stopped you could not get the smile off my face.

From that night I was supernaturally delivered from being an alcoholic, no withdrawals, just totally and instantly set free. Many people can have a drink without becoming an alcoholic, but I would drink most of the time to hide the pain and now that the pain had gone I didn't need or want the alcohol anymore.

I have found out since that this same miraculous "Born Again", experience has happened to countless millions of people right down through history. Many of these people did not need to be delivered from anything, they just knew that there was something missing in their lives, but many others that needed to be set free were instantly delivered of addictions, diseases, grief and scores of other problems, just like I was.

THE PROOF OF THE PUDDING IS IN THE EATING

The "Born Again" experience happens to everyone who accepts Jesus Christ as their Lord and Saviour even when they do not have the same radical experience that I had. What I am saying is that you are no more "Born Again" than anyone else is "Born Again" just because you have a radical conversion. God knows that some people need a radical conversion experience.

The Apostle Paul, or Saint Paul (his name was changed from Saul) as many know Him was one of the most famous Bible characters of all and he had a very similar, yet even more radical experience than myself, but around 2,000 years before me. God says I am the same yesterday, today and forever, so let's have a look at Paul's incredible conversion experience.

Paul was the chief persecutor of Christians and would drag them off to prison, then with his full approval watch as they were killed. Just a couple of scriptures from the Bible to reinforce what a Christian and therefore Jesus despiser Paul once was.

We will begin with a young man by the name of Stephen who was murdered with the full approval of Paul for preaching the Gospel.

> "*57At this they covered their ears and, yelling at the top of their voices, they all rushed at him, 58dragged him out of the city and began to stone him. Meanwhile, the witnesses laid their clothes at the feet of a young man named Saul (Paul). 59While they were stoning him, Stephen prayed, 'Lord Jesus, receive my spirit.' 60Then he fell on his knees and cried out, 'Lord, do not hold this sin against them.' When he had said this, he fell asleep.*"
> Acts 7:57-60

THE KEY TO LIFE

> "[1]*And Saul (Paul) was there, giving approval to his death."*
> Acts 8:1

Paul had spent much of his adult life persecuting Christians for following Jesus and yet one day he was to meet face to face with Jesus Himself. This momentary meeting with Jesus changed Paul in an instant of time and transformed him forever. One encounter or one word spoken to you by Jesus will also change your life forever and you will never be the same either.

I experienced it, millions of others have and around 2,000 years ago so did Paul, as did all the other followers of Jesus. He was the chief amongst the persecutors of Christians and yet Jesus saw something special in him, so by the power of the Holy Spirit He touched him. That touch was so powerful and life changing that Paul was prepared to spend the rest of his life not as the chief persecutor, but as one of the chief persecuted.

Paul was targeted by his people for the rest of his life for becoming a Christian and suffered every possible violent attack you can imagine.

He was beaten, bashed and imprisoned more times than you could count as you will read in these next few pages. During his brief encounter with Jesus he would not only be "Born Again", but called, anointed and appointed by Him to spend the rest of his days preaching the Gospel. There is nothing in the universe that can so powerfully transform you as a touch from God and this is pretty obvious in Paul's case. He was so transformed in an instant that he turned his back on power, reputation, fame and authority. He would now operate in God's authority but would face the same persecution that he inflicted on thousands of Christians and who in their right mind would do that unless they had been truly touched by God.

When I speak about God, Jesus and the Holy Spirit do not get confused as I used to, because The Father, The Son and The Holy Spirit are all one and the same and make up the Trinity. They are all God but they also have different functions and expressions, so let me explain it another way to you. The sun in the sky has three parts to it, the physical sun, the heat and the light, they are all part of the sun but have different expressions. There are thousands and thousands of examples around us of this same occurrence. You are also a three part being, you are a spirit (the real you), you have a soul (your emotions), and you live in a body (the vehicle you get around in) and although each part has a different function and expression the three parts form you. The Bible says in Genesis that God created man in His image and if we are in His image we must have three parts to our being, just like He has or we would not be In His image!

> "[26] *Then God said, 'Let us make man in our image, in our likeness, and let them rule over the fish of the sea and the birds of the air, over the livestock, over all the earth, and over all the creatures that move along the ground.'* [27] *So God created man in his own image, in the image of God he created him; male and female he created them.*"
> Genesis 1:26-27

SAUL (PAUL) MEETS FACE TO FACE WITH JESUS

> "[1] *Meanwhile, Saul was still breathing out murderous threats against the Lord's disciples. He went to the high*

THE KEY TO LIFE

priest ²*and asked him for letters to the synagogues in Damascus, so that if he found any there who belonged to the Way, whether men or women, he might take them as prisoners to Jerusalem.* ³*As he neared Damascus on his journey, suddenly a light from heaven flashed around him.* ⁴*He fell to the ground and heard a voice say to him, 'Saul, Saul, why do you persecute me?'* ⁵ *'Who are you, Lord?' Saul asked. 'I am Jesus, whom you are persecuting,' he replied.* ⁶ *'Now get up and go into the city, and you will be told what you must do.'* ⁷*The men traveling with Saul stood there speechless; they heard the sound but did not see anyone.* ⁸*Saul got up from the ground, but when he opened his eyes he could see nothing. So they led him by the hand into Damascus.* ⁹*For three days he was blind, and did not eat or drink anything.* ¹⁰*In Damascus there was a disciple named Ananias. The Lord called to him in a vision, 'Ananias!' 'Yes, Lord,' he answered.* ¹¹*The Lord told him, 'Go to the house of Judas on Straight Street and ask for a man from Tarsus named Saul, for he is praying.* ¹²*In a vision he has seen a man named Ananias come and place his hands on him to restore his sight.'* ¹³*'Lord,' Ananias answered, 'I have heard many reports about this man and all the harm he has done to your saints in Jerusalem.* ¹⁴*And he has come here with authority from the chief priests to arrest all who call on your name.'* ¹⁵*But the Lord said to Ananias, 'Go! This man is my chosen instrument to carry my name before the Gentiles and their kings and before the people of Israel.* ¹⁶*I will show him how much he must suffer for my name.'* ¹⁷*Then Ananias went to the house and entered it. Placing his hands on Saul, he said, 'Brother Saul, the Lord—Jesus, who appeared to you on the road as you were coming here—has sent me so that you may see again and be filled*

> *with the Holy Spirit.' ¹⁸Immediately, something like scales fell from Saul's eyes, and he could see again. He got up and was baptized, and ¹⁹after taking some food, he regained his strength. Saul spent several days with the disciples in Damascus. At once he began to preach in the synagogues that Jesus is the Son of God. ²¹All those who heard him were astonished and asked, 'Isn't he the man who raised havoc in Jerusalem among those who call on this name? And hasn't he come here to take them as prisoners to the chief priests?' ²²Yet Saul grew more and more powerful and baffled the Jews living in Damascus by proving that Jesus is the Christ."*
> Acts 9:1-22

When I went to that little Church I had never read the Bible and had absolutely no idea or knowledge of what would happen to me that night and nor did Paul as walked on the road to Damascus.

There are several aspects of Paul's conversion which are absolute blueprints of what happened to me and this story about Paul's conversion has been in the Bible for around 2,000 years, but the same power of Jesus that touched Paul 2,000 years ago, touched me and can touch you right now.

Take for instance where Paul suddenly saw a light from Heaven flash around him and he fell to the ground and heard a voice saying, "Saul, Saul, (Paul, Paul), why do you persecute me?" When I met with Jesus that night and the Pastor prayed for me, I was hit with what seemed like a bolt or flash of lightning from Heaven and I like Paul fell to the ground. The presence of God was so overwhelming that I did not want to stand up anymore and that is probably exactly how Paul felt.

You may have seen this happen on television, in Church, or at a Christian Crusade where people just seem to fall over and you may have thought that the Preacher pushed them.

The Preacher does not have the power, the Holy Spirit does and it is in line with God's Word. I know many people that have gone weak at the knees when they meet a new girl or guy, so how much weaker at the knees should you go when you meet the Creator of the entire universe and He touches you with His power.

Unlike Paul I did not hear an audible voice that night but I have on two occasions since and just like Paul was totally changed in an instant.

Just as Paul knew that it was Jesus who touched him, so did I and yet neither of us knew Him before. When Paul was slain in the Spirit and fell to the ground, he said "Who are you, Lord"? Jesus never told Paul who He was before He touched him, so how did Paul know the voice was the Lord. Paul knew this was the Lord by divine revelation and that is exactly how I knew and how you will know also.

Just a little aside for a moment, I don't know about you but if I was Jesus and had His power I would not have touched Paul with my love and glory, I would have smacked him up the side of the head for what he had done to my people.

It is very a good thing that we humans are not God, because at our worst moments there would be nobody still living would there?

Imagine what you would do if you were God and someone cut you off in the traffic on your way to work, or any other situation that challenges your patience, anyway just a thought, now back to business.

THE PROOF OF THE PUDDING IS IN THE EATING

The Bible speaks about revelation but here we are not talking about the last book of the Bible, which is called The Book of Revelation, we are actually talking about divine revelation from God which is His revealed word to man by the Holy Spirit.

A word, a thought, a scripture, a dream or a vision which comes by revelation from the Holy Spirit is absolutely life changing and is best explained this way. A revelation from The Holy Spirit is "receiving a truth that you would never have found out or would never have known by yourself," because it was conceived in the throne room of God and then by divine revelation birthed in your heart.

It is like that gut feeling you get, an inner knowing, but 100 times more convincing and powerful. When this revelation is from God and not just your own thoughts it is never, ever wrong.

That is why both Paul and I knew it was Jesus Christ that touched us, because it was revealed by the Holy Spirit and not by man.

Being "Born Again" or being saved literally means to be made anew and it is a free gift from God. Because it is a free gift you cannot earn it, perform for it, buy it, barter for it, threaten someone for it, steal it or get it from anywhere else except from God.

You cannot gatecrash Heaven, it is by invitation only and the great news is that everyone is invited. All people that are invited to weddings, parties and the like don't always end up going and sadly not everyone that is invited to the eternal life party accepts the free invitation either. If you do accept you must make sure that you RSVP (accept the invitation) before you die, because once you have died it is too late, the party is over for you.

I can walk up to you in the street and offer you a free motor car but that does not mean that you will accept it and yet you not accepting my gift does not stop it from being a gift.

I know many people that have been significantly touched and even miraculously healed and delivered in the name of Jesus, yet they did not accept Him as their Lord and Saviour, simply because of their pride.

That is why the Bible says that pride always comes before a fall, please don't be one of these people, drop your pride and ask Him to come and live in your heart.

If myself and around 1.5 billion other Christians on earth are wrong about needing to be "Born Again", which has totally transformed our lives, allowing us to live a life of joy, hope, peace, vision, power and passion, we have absolutely nothing to lose. If we are right and the "proof of the pudding is in the eating" and you do not accept Jesus into your life, then you have everything to lose.

Paul was famous and was respected as he encouraged all to persecute Christians, but now that Paul was "Born Again" he was fully aware that he was about to reap exactly what he had sowed. He was however so transformed, that he was compelled to share this incredible new life with all who would listen. He believed the temporary pain he was about to endure was worth it, because of the incredible eternal future that he and all who accepted Jesus would enjoy for all eternity.

Before we have a look at what Paul went through we must realize that Paul did not have to accept Jesus into his life that day and he also did not have to accept the call Jesus put on his life to preach the Gospel, however if he had not accepted the commission then we may never have heard this life changing message. The free gift of salvation would have still been there but who would have shared it with us? I am sure God would have raised somebody else up to do it, but I for one will certainly be thanking Paul when I get to heaven.

PAUL FLOGGED AND IMPRISONED

> "*¹He came to Derbe and then to Lystra, where a disciple named Timothy lived, whose mother was a Jewess and a believer, but whose father was a Greek. ²The brothers at Lystra and Iconium spoke well of*
>
> *him. ³Paul wanted to take him along on the journey, so he circumcised him because of the Jews who lived in that area, for they all knew that his father was a Greek. ⁴As they traveled from town to town, they delivered the decisions reached by the apostles and elders in Jerusalem for the people to obey. ⁵So the churches were strengthened in the faith and grew daily in numbers.*
>
> *⁶Paul and his companions traveled throughout the region of Phrygia and Galatia, having been kept by the Holy Spirit from preaching the word in the province of Asia. ⁷When they came to the border of Mysia, they tried to enter Bithynia, but the Spirit of Jesus would not allow them to. ⁸So they passed by Mysia and went down to Troas. ⁹During the night Paul had a vision of a man of Macedonia standing and begging him, 'Come over to Macedonia and help us.' ¹⁰After Paul had seen the*

vision, we got ready at once to leave for Macedonia, concluding that God had called us to preach the gospel to them."

" ¹¹From Troas we put out to sea and sailed straight for Samothrace, and the next day on to Neapolis. "¹²From there we traveled to Philippi, a Roman colony and the leading city of that district of Macedonia. And we stayed there several days."

" ¹³On the Sabbath we went outside the city gate to the river, where we expected to find a place of prayer. We sat down and began to speak to the women who had gathered there. ¹⁴One of those listening was a woman named Lydia, a dealer in purple cloth from the city of Thyatira, who was a worshiper of God. The Lord opened her heart to respond to Paul's message. ¹⁵When she and the members of her household were baptized, she invited us to her home. 'If you consider me a believer in the Lord,' she said, 'come and stay at my house.' And she persuaded us."

" ¹⁶Once when we were going to the place of prayer, we were met by a slave girl who had a spirit by which she predicted the future. She earned a great deal of money for her owners by fortune-telling. ¹⁷This girl followed Paul and the rest of us, shouting, 'These men are servants of the Most High God, who are telling you the way to be saved.' ¹⁸She kept this up for many days. Finally Paul became so troubled that he turned around and said to the spirit, 'In the name of Jesus Christ I command you to come out of her!' At that moment the spirit left her."

" ¹⁹When the owners of the slave girl realized that their

hope of making money was gone, they seized Paul and Silas and dragged them into the marketplace to face the authorities. ²⁰They brought them before the magistrates and said, 'These men are Jews, and are throwing our city into an uproar ²¹by advocating customs unlawful for us Romans to accept or practice.' ²²The crowd joined in the attack against Paul and Silas, and the magistrates ordered them to be stripped and beaten. ²³After they had been severely flogged, they were thrown into prison, and the jailer was commanded to guard them carefully."

" ²⁴Upon receiving such orders, he put them in the inner cell and fastened their feet in the stocks. ²⁵About midnight Paul and Silas were praying and singing hymns to God, and the other prisoners were listening to them. ²⁶Suddenly there was such a violent earthquake that the foundations of the prison were shaken. At once all the prison doors flew open, and everybody's chains came loose. ²⁷The jailer woke up, and when he saw the prison doors open, he drew his sword and was about to kill himself because he thought the prisoners had escaped."

" ²⁸But Paul shouted, 'Don't harm yourself! We are all here!' ²⁹The jailer called for lights, rushed in and fell trembling before Paul and Silas. ³⁰He then brought them out and asked, 'Sirs, what must I do to be saved?' ³¹They replied, 'Believe in the Lord Jesus, and you will be saved—you and your household.' ³²Then they spoke the word of the Lord to him and to all the others in his house. ³³At that hour of the night the jailer took them and washed their wounds; then immediately he and all his family were baptized. ³⁴The jailer brought them into his house and set a meal before them; he was filled with joy because he had come to

believe in God—he and his whole family."

" ³⁵When it was daylight, the magistrates sent their officers to the jailer with the order: 'Release those men.' ³⁶The jailer told Paul, 'The magistrates have ordered that you and Silas be released. Now you can leave. Go in peace.' ³⁷But Paul said to the officers: 'They beat us publicly without a trial, even though we are Roman citizens, and threw us into prison. And now do they want to get rid of us quietly? No! Let them come themselves and escort us out.' ³⁸The officers reported this to the magistrates, and when they heard that Paul and Silas were Roman citizens, they were alarmed. ³⁹They came to appease them and escorted them from the prison, requesting them to leave the city. ⁴⁰After Paul and Silas came out of the prison, they went to Lydia's house, where they met with the brothers and encouraged them. Then they left."
Acts 16:1-40

PLOT TO KILL PAUL

"¹Paul looked straight at the Sanhedrin and said, 'My brothers, I have fulfilled my duty to God in all good conscience to this day.' ²At this the high priest Ananias ordered those standing near Paul to strike him on the mouth. ³Then Paul said to him, 'God will strike you, you white-washed wall! You sit there to judge me according to the law, yet you yourself violate the law by commanding that I be struck!' ⁴Those who were standing near Paul said, 'You dare to insult God's high priest?' ⁵Paul replied, 'Brothers, I did not realize that he was the high priest; for it is written: 'Do not speak evil about the ruler of your people.'"

"⁶Then Paul, knowing that some of them were Sadducees and the others Pharisees, called out in the Sanhedrin, 'My brothers, I am a Pharisee, the son of a Pharisee. I stand on trial because of my hope in the resurrection of the dead.' ⁷When he said this, a dispute broke out between the Pharisees and the Sadducees, and the assembly was divided. ⁸(The Sadducees say that there is no resurrection, and that there are neither angels nor spirits, but the Pharisees acknowledge them all.)"

"⁹There was a great uproar and some of the teachers of the law who were Pharisees stood up and argued vigorously. 'We find nothing wrong with this man,' they said. 'What if a spirit or an angel has spoken to him?' ¹⁰The dispute became so violent that the commander was afraid Paul would be torn to pieces by them. He ordered the troops to go down and take him away from them by force and bring him into the barracks."

"¹¹The following night the Lord stood near Paul and said, 'Take courage! As you have testified about me in Jerusalem, so you must also testify in Rome.' ¹²The next morning the Jews formed a conspiracy and bound themselves with an oath not to eat or drink until they had killed Paul. ¹³More than forty men were involved in this plot. ¹⁴They went to the chief priests and elders and said, 'We have taken a solemn oath not to eat anything until we have killed Paul. ¹⁵Now then, you and the Sanhedrin petition the commander to bring him before you on the pretext of wanting more accurate information about his case. We are ready to kill him before he gets here.' ¹⁶But when the son of Paul's sister heard of this plot, he went into the barracks and told Paul. ¹⁷Then Paul called one of the centurions and said, 'Take this young man to the commander; he has something to tell him.' ¹⁸So he took him to the commander. The centurion said, 'Paul, the prisoner, sent for me and asked me to bring this young man to you because he has something to tell you.'"

"¹⁹The commander took the young man by the hand, drew him aside and asked, 'What is it you want to tell me?' ²⁰He said: 'The Jews have agreed to ask you to bring Paul before the Sanhedrin tomorrow on the pretext of wanting more accurate information about him. ²¹Don't give in to them, because more than forty of them are waiting in ambush for him. They have taken an oath not to eat or drink until they have killed him. They are ready now, waiting for your consent to their request.'"

"²²The commander dismissed the young man and cautioned him, 'Don't tell anyone that you have reported this to me.' ²³Then he called two of his centurions and ordered them, 'Get ready a detachment of two hundred soldiers, seventy horsemen and two hundred spearmen to go to Caesarea at nine tonight. ²⁴Provide mounts for Paul so that he may be taken safely to Governor Felix.' ²⁵He wrote a letter as follows: '²⁶Claudius Lysias, To His Excellency, Governor Felix: Greetings.'"

"'²⁷This man was seized by the Jews and they were about to kill him, but I came with my troops and rescued him, for I had learned that he is a Roman citizen. ²⁸I wanted to know why they were accusing him, so I brought him to their Sanhedrin. ²⁹I found that the accusation had to do with questions about their law, but there was no charge

> *against him that deserved death or imprisonment.* ³⁰*When I was informed of a plot to be carried out against the man, I sent him to you at once. I also ordered his accusers to present to you their case against him.'* ³¹*So the soldiers, carrying out their orders, took Paul with them during the night and brought him as far as Antipatris.* ³²*The next day they let the cavalry go on with him, while they returned to the barracks."*
>
> "³³*When the cavalry arrived in Caesarea, they delivered the letter to the governor and handed Paul over to him.* ³⁴*The governor read the letter and asked what province he was from. Learning that he was from Cilicia,* ³⁵*he said, 'I will hear your case when your accusers get here.'"*
>
> " *Then he ordered that Paul be kept under guard in Herod's palace. Paul was once again released, Jesus had things for Paul to do and until his destiny on this earth was fulfilled no man would be able to kill him no matter how they tried."*
> Acts 23:1-35

It has been said that there are currently around 330,000 Christians around the world every year that are killed for preaching the name of Jesus.

Don't believe just what you can see and hear, start thinking about believing in what you can't see, make an informed decision because your life tomorrow depends on your decisions today and that includes your eternal life.

Your spirit, the real you, does not die when you do, it cannot be killed, it will live forever and the important thing is where will you live?

How do you make an informed decision? I have said it many times, "the proof of the pudding is in the eating." Cry out to God right where you are now and ask Jesus to come and live in your heart and He will do just that, or if you would prefer and you are able, go to a Church that preaches salvation through Jesus and you will changed forever just like me, Paul and millions of others.

When a woman conceives and has a baby living inside her she knows a long time before she ever sees and meets her child that she is pregnant.

When you accept Jesus Christ as your Lord and Saviour you will know that He is living inside you a long time before you will actually meet Him face to face in heaven.

It is amazing how people have no problem believing in things they can't see when it suits them, like radio waves, wind, spoken words, gravity, sperm cells, the human spirit and millions of other unseen things that are around them.

You might argue that although you cannot see these things, you can see or feel the evidence or the impact they have on you and so let me introduce you to several hundred thousand Christians that were once alcoholics, prostitutes, bank robbers, prisoners serving life, mentally insane, murderers, lepers, patients with terminal cancer, blind, victims of AIDS and many other terminal diseases, cripples, gang leaders, abused children, mentally tormented, satanists, witch doctors, demoniacs, off the planet religious fanatics, millionaires with no joy, world heavy weight boxing champions that felt empty, grand slam tennis champions, (one that publicly after winning the French Open and in front of a television audience reported to have been around 1.5 billion people thanked Jesus for everything he has done, everything that he is and that without Him he was nothing), a reformed alcoholic world cup championship winning rugby union player, leaders of nations that were a mess, motivational speakers that were once on the scrap heap (including me), preachers that had terminal diseases as children and one in particular that said to God if He would heal him, he would serve Him for the rest his life and he still is. He was healed of tuberculosis at 17 years of age when he was given 4 months to live. As a young Christian girl prayed for him he was totally healed which dumbfounded his family and the medical profession.

This awesome man of God by the name of Doctor David Yonggi Cho now has the largest Church in the history of the earth, in Seoul Korea with around 800,000 members.

Doctor Cho honoured his commitment to serve God, and now with Jesus, the Holy Spirit and the whole of Heaven on his side has literally changed the face of an entire Nation.

If that is not the evidence of things unseen changing and having incredible impact on that which is seen, then what is?

In fact there is a scripture in the Bible designed for this very purpose and it can be found in the book of Hebrews in the New Testament.

> "*¹Now faith is being sure of what we hope for and certain of what we do not see. ²This is what the ancients were commended for. ³By faith we understand that the universe was formed at God's command, so that what is seen was not made out of what was visible.*"
> Hebrews 11:1

Most of us believe that the human spirit lives in us, but the spirit of God living in us, how could that be? If we can't believe this, then there is something terribly wrong with our belief system. It is "FAITH" that the Kingdom of God operates within, but we have been educated that when we see it we will believe, yet we believe in all these other things that we cannot see except God, I just don't get it!

Once again faith says, not seeing is still believing.

THE HOLY SPIRIT COMES, TO START THE CHURCH

> *"¹When the day of Pentecost came; they were all together in one place. ²Suddenly a sound like the blowing of a violent wind came from heaven and filled the whole house where they were sitting. ³They saw what seemed to be tongues of fire that separated and came to rest on each of them. ⁴All of them were filled with the Holy Spirit and began to speak in other tongues as the Spirit enabled them. ⁵Now there were staying in Jerusalem God-fearing Jews from every nation under heaven. ⁶When they heard this sound, a crowd came together in bewilderment, because each one heard them speaking in his own language. ⁷Utterly amazed, they asked: 'Are not all these men who are speaking Galileans? ⁸Then how is it that each of us hears them in his own native language? ⁹Parthians, Medes and Elamites; residents of Mesopotamia, Judea and Cappadocia, Pontus and Asia, ¹⁰Phrygia and Pamphylia, Egypt and the parts of Libya near Cyrene; visitors from Rome ¹¹(both Jews and converts to Judaism); Cretans and Arabs—we hear them declaring the wonders of God in our own tongues!'"*

" [12]*Amazed and perplexed, they asked one another, 'What does this mean?'* [13]*Some, however, made fun of them and said, 'They have had too much wine.'* [14]*Then Peter stood up with the Eleven, raised his voice and addressed the crowd: 'Fellow Jews and all of you who live in Jerusalem, let me explain this to you; listen carefully to what I say.* [15]*These men are not drunk, as you suppose. It's only nine in the morning!* [16]*No, this is what was spoken by the prophet Joel:* " [17]*In the last days, God says, I will pour out my Spirit on all people. Your sons and daughters will prophesy, your young men will see visions, your old men will dream dreams.* [18]*Even on my servants, both men and women, I will pour out my Spirit in those days, and they will prophesy.* [19]*I will show wonders in the heaven above and signs on the earth below, blood and fire and billows of smoke.* [20]*The sun will be turned to darkness and the moon to blood before the coming of the great and glorious day of the Lord.* [21]*And everyone who calls on the name of the Lord will be saved.'"*

"[22]*Men of Israel, listen to this: Jesus of Nazareth was a man accredited by God to you by miracles, wonders and signs, which God did among you through him, as you yourselves know.* [23]*This man was handed over to you by God's set purpose and foreknowledge; and you, with the help of wicked men, put him to death by nailing him to the cross.* [24]*But God raised him from the dead, freeing him from the agony of death, because it was impossible for death to keep its hold on him.* [25]*David said about him: 'I saw the Lord always before me. Because he is at my right hand, I will not be shaken.* [26]*Therefore my heart is glad and my tongue rejoices; my body also will live in hope,* [27]*because you will not abandon me to the grave,* nor will you let your Holy One see decay. ²⁸You have made known to me the paths of life; you will fill me with joy in your presence.'"

"²⁹Brothers, I can tell you confidently that the patriarch David died and was buried, and his tomb is here to this day. ³⁰But he was a prophet and knew that God had promised him on oath that he

would place one of his descendants on his throne. ³¹Seeing what was ahead, he spoke of the resurrection of the Christ, that he was not abandoned to the grave, nor did his body see decay. ³²God has raised

this Jesus to life, and we are all witnesses of the fact. ³³Exalted to the right hand of God, he has received from the Father the promised Holy Spirit and has poured out what you now see and hear. ³⁴For David did not ascend to heaven, and yet he said, 'The Lord said to my Lord: "Sit at my right hand ³⁵ until I make your enemies a footstool for your feet."'

" ³⁶Therefore let all Israel be assured of this: God has made this Jesus, whom you crucified, both Lord and Christ." ³⁷When the people heard this, they were cut to the heart and said to Peter and the other apostles, 'Brothers, what shall we do?' ³⁸Peter replied, 'Repent and be baptized, every one of you, in the name of Jesus Christ for the forgiveness of your sins. And you will receive the gift of the Holy Spirit. ³⁹The promise is for you and your children and for all who are far off—for all whom the Lord our God will call.' (That's you and me) ⁴⁰With many other words he warned them; and he pleaded with them, 'Save

> *yourselves from this corrupt generation.' ⁴¹Those who accepted his message were baptized, and about three thousand were added to their number that day. ⁴²They devoted themselves to the apostles' teaching and to the fellowship, to the breaking of bread and to prayer.*
>
> *⁴³Everyone was filled with awe, and many wonders and miraculous signs were done by the apostles. ⁴⁴All the believers were together and had everything in common. ⁴⁵Selling their possessions and goods, they gave to anyone as he had need. ⁴⁶Every day they continued to meet together in the temple courts. They broke bread in their homes and ate together with glad and sincere hearts, ⁴⁷praising God and enjoying the favor of all the people. And the Lord added to their number daily those who were being saved."*
> Acts 2:1-47

That which was written in the Bible over 2, 000 years ago that saved Paul, the disciples and 100's of millions of people down through the centuries happened for me and can happen for you. You may be just like I was and have no idea of what the Bible says, well the great news is that you don't need to know what it says just put your trust in God and pray the prayer that I prayed and you will be saved.

PAUL SHARES HIS TESTIMONY

Paul is no longer called Saul and this story is after his conversion, it takes place in a courtroom when he was facing charges for preaching.

"¹Then Agrippa said to Paul, 'You have permission to speak for yourself.' So Paul motioned with his hand and began his defense: ² 'King Agrippa, I consider myself fortunate to stand before you today as I make my defense against all the accusations of the Jews, ³and especially so because you are well acquainted with all the Jewish customs and controversies. Therefore, I beg you to listen to me patiently. ⁴"The Jews all know the way I have lived ever since I was a child, from the beginning of my life in my own country, and also in Jerusalem. ⁵They have known me for a long time and can testify, if they are willing, that according to the strictest sect of our religion, I lived as a Pharisee.'"

" '⁶And now it is because of my hope in what God has promised our fathers that I am on trial today. ⁷This is the promise our twelve tribes are hoping to see fulfilled as they earnestly serve God day and night. O king, it is because of this hope that the Jews are accusing me. ⁸Why should any of you consider it incredible that God raises the dead? ⁹I too was convinced that I ought to do all that was possible to oppose the name of Jesus of Nazareth. ¹⁰And that is just what I did in Jerusalem. On the authority of the chief priests I put many of the saints in prison, and when they were put to death, I cast my vote against them. ¹¹Many a time I went from one synagogue to another to have them punished, and I tried to force them to blaspheme. In my obsession against them, I even went to foreign cities to persecute them.'"

"'¹²On one of these journeys I was going to Damascus with the authority and commission of the chief priests. ¹³About noon, O king, as I was on the road, I saw a light from

heaven, brighter than the sun, blazing around me and my companions. ¹⁴We all fell to the ground, and I heard a voice saying to me in Aramaic, "Saul, Saul, why do you persecute me? It is hard for you to kick against the goads."

"¹⁵Then I asked, 'Who are you, Lord?' 'I am Jesus, whom you are persecuting,' the Lord replied. ¹⁶'Now get up and stand on your feet. I have appeared to you to appoint you as a servant and as a witness of what you have seen of me and what I will show you. ¹⁷I will rescue you from your own people and from the Gentiles. I am sending you to them ¹⁸to open their eyes and turn them from darkness to light, and from the power of Satan to God, so that they may receive forgiveness of sins and a place among those who are sanctified by faith in me.' ' ¹⁹So then, King Agrippa, I was not disobedient to the vision from heaven. ²⁰First to those in Damascus, then to those in Jerusalem and in all Judea, and to the Gentiles also, I preached that they should repent and turn to God and prove their repentance by their deeds. ²¹That is why the Jews seized me in the temple courts and tried to kill me.

²²But I have had God's help to this very day, and so I stand here and testify to small and great alike. I am saying nothing beyond what the prophets and Moses said would happen—²³that the Christ would suffer and, as the first to rise from the dead, would proclaim light to his own people and to the Gentiles."

" ²⁴At this point Festus interrupted Paul's defense. 'You are out of your mind, Paul!' he shouted. 'Your great learning is driving you insane.' ' ²⁵I am not insane, most excellent Festus,' Paul replied. 'What I am saying is true and rea-

sonable. ²⁶*The king is familiar with these things, and I can speak freely to him. I am convinced that none of this has escaped his notice, because it was not done in a corner.* ²⁷*King Agrippa, do you believe the prophets? I know you do.'* ²⁸*Then Agrippa said to Paul, 'Do you think that in such a short time you can persuade me to be a Christian?'* ²⁹*Paul replied, 'Short time or long—I pray God that not only you but all who are listening to me today may become what I am, except for these chains.'* ³⁰*The king rose, and with him the governor and Bernice and those sitting with them.* ³¹*They left the room, and while talking with one another, they said, 'This man is not doing anything that deserves death or imprisonment.'"*
Acts 26: 1-31

PAUL'S FINAL WORDS ABOUT RUNNING THE RACE

This is Paul speaking at the end of his ministry and just prior to his death.

> "*¹In the presence of God and of Christ Jesus, who will judge the living and the dead, and in view of his appearing and his kingdom, I give you this charge: ²Preach the Word; be prepared in season and out of season; correct, rebuke and encourage—with great patience and careful instruction. ³For the time will come when men will not put up with sound doctrine. Instead, to suit their own desires, they will gather around them a great number of teachers to say what their itching ears want to hear. ⁴They will turn their ears away from the truth and turn aside to myths. ⁵But you, keep your head in all situations, endure hardship, do the work of an evangelist, discharge all the duties of your ministry. ⁶For I am already being*

> *poured out like a drink offering, and the time has come for my departure. ⁷I have fought the good fight, I have finished the race, I have kept the faith. ⁸Now there is in store for me the crown of righteousness, which the Lord, the righteous Judge, will award to me on that day—and not only to me, but also to all who have longed for His appearing..."*
> 2 Timothy 1-8

There it is right there, run the race, because you were Born a Winner, to Live a Winner and to Die a Winner.

> *"¹⁷But the Lord stood at my side and gave me strength, so that through me the message might be fully proclaimed and all the Gentiles might hear it. And I was delivered from the lion's mouth. ¹⁸The Lord will rescue me from every evil attack and will bring me safely to His heavenly kingdom. To him be glory for ever and ever. Amen."*
> 2 Timothy 17-18

We cannot see Jesus right now, we also cannot see the wind but we can experience and feel Him, just as we can experience and feel the wind.

Not only that but we can see and experience what the wind does, just as we can see and experience what Jesus will do in our lives. I have seen thousands of lives transformed after surrendering their lives to Jesus and when you have invited Him into your life you will know, that you know, that you know, that you are saved and Heaven bound when you die, just as Paul has just said.

All of a sudden the Bible stops being just a book and it becomes alive to you, just as the blood stream is the internal river of life for our physical lives, the Bible becomes our river of life for our spiritual lives.

If you were to read every motivation book that was ever written you would find that every proven strategy for success was already written in the Bible years before the author of that motivation book was ever born. The author either stumbled on them by accident, read them in the Bible or read someone else's book who got them from the Bible.

The Bible contains God's universal laws from Genesis to Revelation and the only way we will ever experience true success, is by obeying God's Word and universal laws He put into place, whether we are obeying them consciously or unconsciously.

True success cannot be measured only by what happens in this life, because to be the most successful person in your chosen field in the history of the earth in this life and then miss out on Heaven would be earthly success that ended in eternal failure.

We have talked much about the law of sowing and reaping and that is the exact law that Jesus Himself had to obey for us to receive forgiveness of our sins and to gain eternal life.

Jesus sowed his life so that He could reap our lives and that was the only way that the law of sin and death could be overcome. Someone had to die for the sin of the world so God Himself in the person of Jesus came to earth to die because of what His own law said.

I don't know about you but if I had His power I think while nobody was looking I would change the law, so that I didn't have to suffer the pain and humiliation of being crucified.

THE PROOF OF THE PUDDING IS IN THE EATING

Jesus did not change the law to suit His own agenda, but followed through and died for our sin and I hope you are now convinced about how much He loves you.

Jesus only had one life to sow, but just like other seeds that are sown they multiply at harvest time and today that seed which was His life has reaped around one and a half thousand million lives that are actually living today and that does not include the billions that are already in Heaven with Him.

If Jesus had not sown his life then He would not have been able to firstly overcome the law of sin and death and secondly reap our lives. He did not have to die for our sin and was never forced to by the Father. Just like you and me He had a free will, but Jesus exercised that free will and made a decision to die on the cross for you. You are now free to make a decision to except Him as your Lord and Saviour, He will not make that decision for you, it is a free gift and you can accept it or reject it, but please do not be seen dead without Him in your life.

CHAPTER NINE
BORN ONCE, DIE A LOSER
BORN TWICE, DIE A WINNER

I am so excited to finally be able to share this part of the story with you because it started nearly 7 years ago when the Lord showed me a vision one night after Church. I was lying in my bed and I would never have known many of the things written in this book unless the Holy Spirit had actually revealed them to me. When God speaks it can be audibly, it can be by revelation from His Word, through the mouth of a prophet, by way of vision, in a dream either awake or asleep, He could send an angel to you, transport you to Heaven, or He could appear in front of you and many people have had that incredible experience, or if He really wanted to He could drive up your driveway, knock on your door and tell you in person.

Whatever way God speaks to you will change your life forever and you will never be the same.

Being "Born Again", is experienced by His divine intervention and then knowing that you are "Born Again" is experienced by His divine revelation, it is a knowing, that you know, that you know, that you are saved.

That night after Church as I lay on my bed thinking about lost people and the miracle of the second birth, I asked the Holy Spirit to show me why He called this miracle second birth, "Born Again" and asked if He would teach me all about it, so that I could write this book to show you that He was the author of two births.

What He showed me in a vision over the next two or three hours was incredible and so overwhelmed was I, that I just lay there and wept the whole time.

He showed me the amazing parallel and relationship between our natural conception and our natural birth and our spiritual conception and our spiritual birth. They are so similar that they are a blue print of each another and this leads to one conclusion, both births are imperative and they have the one and the same author, God!

You would not argue with the fact that you needed to have a natural birth or you would not have been born into the world. You can however argue about the need to have a second birth but God says that without it you cannot be born into His Kingdom and go to heaven. This chapter will show you beyond any shadow of doubt that God planned both births and that because you have experienced the first one, you now need to experience the second one and when you do you will be born into eternity.

If we only needed to be born once then God would have stopped at one. He is not stupid you know, mind you I have met a few people that think God should have waited for them to be born before He made any decisions, you might know a few too.

The Bible is the number one selling book in the world every year and it is amazing that we hardly ever see it advertised. Now from God's Word The Bible, I want to show you how God planned for you not only to have a natural birth and receive His free gift of this life, but how He also planned for you to have a spiritual birth, to receive His free gift of eternal life.

As we have established the Bible talks about the need to be "Born Again" and in the following scriptures we will see a conversation between Jesus and Nicodemus who was one of the most powerful and influential men in the known world during that time. This conversation could be likened to you having a conversation with the President or the Prime Minister of your Nation.

If you are reading this book and are the President or a Prime Minister of a Nation I am not suggesting that you are having a conversation with yourself, however I would imagine that you often feel like you are talking to yourself when trying to gather support from some of your people.

Nicodemus was obviously lost and searching for THE KEY TO LIFE and so he came to Jesus. He came at night and this was probably to avoid being seen, so that his reputation with the people would not be at risk, after all aren't the leaders of the nation expected to have it all together and know all the answers. Try asking some and they will tell you that they need all the help they can get, just like you and me. President Abraham Lincoln was reported to have said something like this. "I had so many decisions to make on a daily basis as the leader of one of the greatest nations in the world that I had only one place to go, to my knees!"

It is very hard to stumble when you are on your knees and because we have entered the electronic age God has decided to keep up with times, so you can now contact him by, KNEEMAIL.

THE NEED TO BE BORN AGAIN

> "*¹Now there was a man of the Pharisees named Nicodemus, a member of the Jewish ruling council. ²He came to Jesus at night and said, 'Rabbi, we know you are a teacher who has come from God. For no one could perform the miraculous signs you are doing if God were not with him.' ³In reply Jesus declared, 'I tell you the truth, no one can see the kingdom of God unless he is born again.'"*

> "*⁴How can a man be born when he is old?' Nicodemus asked. 'Surely he cannot enter a second time into his mother's womb to be born!' ⁵Jesus answered, 'I tell you the truth, no one can enter the kingdom of God unless he is born of water and the Spirit. ⁶Flesh gives birth to flesh, but the Spirit gives birth to spirit. ⁷You should not be surprised at my saying, "You must be born again." ⁸The wind blows wherever it pleases. You hear its sound, but you cannot tell where it comes from or where it is going. So it is with everyone born of the Spirit.' ⁹ How can this be?' Nicodemus asked. ' ¹⁰You are Israel's teacher,' said Jesus, 'and do you not understand these things?'"*

> "*¹¹I tell you the truth, we speak of what we know, and we*

testify to what we have seen, but still you people do not accept our testimony. ¹²I have spoken to you of earthly things and you do not believe; how then will you believe if I speak of heavenly things? ¹³No one has ever gone into heaven except the one who came from heaven—the Son of Man. ¹⁴Just as Moses lifted up the snake in the desert, so the Son of Man must be lifted up, ¹⁵that everyone who believes in him may have eternal life.'"

"'¹⁶For God so loved the world that he gave his one and only Son, that whoever believes in him shall not perish but have eternal life. ¹⁷For God did not send his Son into the world to condemn the world, but to save the world through him. ¹⁸Whoever believes in him is not condemned, but whoever does not believe stands condemned already because he has not believed in the name of God's one and only Son.'"

"'¹⁹This is the verdict: Light has come into the world, but men loved darkness instead of light because their deeds were evil. ²⁰Everyone who does evil hates the light, and will not come into the light for fear that his deeds will be exposed. ²¹But whoever lives by the truth comes into the light, so that it may be seen plainly that what he has done has been done through God.'"

"'³¹The one who comes from above is above all; the one who is from the earth belongs to the earth, and speaks as one from the earth. The one who comes from heaven is above all. ³²He testifies to what he has seen and heard, but no one accepts his testimony. ³³The man who has accepted it has certified that God is truthful. ³⁴For the one whom God has sent speaks the words of God, for God gives the

> Spirit without limit. ³⁵The Father loves the Son and has placed everything in his hands. ³⁶Whoever believes in the Son has eternal life, but whoever rejects the Son will not see life, for God's wrath remains on him.'"
> John 3:1-21, 31-36

In the book of Psalms when God was speaking by the Holy Spirit through King David, He was also speaking this prophetic word to you and me.

> "¹³For you created my inmost being; you knit me together in my mother's womb. ¹⁴I praise you because I am fearfully and wonderfully made; your works are wonderful, I know that full well. ¹⁵My frame was not hidden from you when I was made in the secret place. When I was woven together in the depths of the earth, ¹⁶your eyes saw my unformed body. All the days ordained for me were written in your book before one of them came to be."
> Psalm 139:13-16

YOUR NATURAL BIRTH SUMMARY

We spoke in chapter one and I would like to give you a quick reminder here, millions of sperm cells were released into the reproductive tract of your mother and yet it only took one of these sperm to make her pregnant and to create you.

When you were a sperm cell you were only half the person you are now and half the person that you needed to be. You as a sperm cell had to diligently seek out your other half, which was the egg cell in your mother's fallopian tube, which is right up at the highest point of her reproductive tract. This caused you to swim often directly upstream, that is directly towards the sky if your mother was walking around any of the time. You had to swim for up to 36 hours and as far as 147 kilometres or around 80 miles in human ratio terms to reach the egg cell and so well done you ultra marathon athlete.

You won and therefore David in the Bible was correct in what he prophesied under the inspiration of the Holy Spirit, you must have also been the chosen one to win this race before the foundation of the earth was laid, WOW!!!

After writing about sperm cells much earlier in this book that turn around and attack other sperm that are swimming toward the egg cell, I have since spoken to a microbiologist who said there may be reason to believe that a path seems to be cleared through the middle of the remaining sperm, for particular sperm to travel through undisturbed to reach the egg cell.

It must have happened because you made it, which could mean, he is right. You were a champion swimmer, and God protected his chosen one from being destroyed by the other sperm.

Prophecy is God inspired words spoken by man but under the inspiration of the Holy Spirit and the easiest way for me to explain it, is that when I speak out a prophesy it feels almost like God has borrowed my mouth, my spirit, and my mind for a time. Godly prophecy is a miracle because it comes straight from God and when the person who is being prophesied over hears it they are changed in an instant. If you receive a prophecy it should only ever confirm what is already in your heart.

There are many people that mean well, like those who read palms, crystal balls and the like, but that is not God's way of speaking to His people.

God always sends a man or woman of God to speak His prophetic word and prophecy unlike forms of fortune telling is not negative or trying to speak to the dead.

The Bible says it should be edifying, encouraging and uplifting even when the word may challenge you on an area of your life that you need to get right, it should always contain the truth (the truth is not always just facts) and the truth will always set you free. If it is not confirming something that is already in your heart and is not spoken by a mature balanced Christian then you need to put it on the shelf and seek Godly counsel from your Pastor.

By virtue of the fact that you were born you must have aligned yourself with what the Word of God said about you being the chosen one and you may have been unaware of it until right now. The bottom line is that you were chosen and you won, however nothing is ever that easy. You had to choose to run the race in the first place or you could never have won it. The human race is no different, you can win it but first you must choose to run with purpose and a never give up attitude.

At the end of your race in the womb you were united with your other half the egg and then the two of you became one person. You spent around 3 days in the fallopian tube where you were conceived and then at the right time travelled into the womb where you would grow and stay until your birth. The womb is where the blood stream of your mother delivered to you all the necessary nutrients, oxygen and other things you needed to prosper and develop whilst in her womb. Your mother's blood stream did not only deliver but it also took away, which is very important, as we will discover when we look at the spiritual birth parallel. The blood stream of your mother and your blood stream were completely separate and this is also very important to understand and remember, as you will discover later.

Many people assume that mother and baby are actually joined physically together and that they share the same blood stream, but this is not the case.

You were never connected directly to your mother or her blood stream and were separated by what is called a semi permeable membrane, which is like being separated by a piece of pliable plastic or a type of glad wrap or something of that nature. You may have been able to feel her movements, her warmth and her vibrations but you were never actually touching skin to skin. The way your mother delivered your food, your oxygen and at the same took away your waste products such as carbon dioxide and the like was by an incredible process called osmosis.

OSMOSIS

If two solutions of different concentration are separated by a semi-permeable membrane which is permeable to the smaller solvent molecules but not to the larger solute molecules, then the solvent will tend to diffuse across the membrane from the less concentrated to the more concentrated solution, this process is called osmosis. Osmosis is of great importance in biological processes where the solvent is water. The transport of water and other molecules across biological membranes is essential to many processes in living organisms.

The energy which drives the process is usually discussed in terms of osmotic pressure.

This incredible and miraculous process caused transference to take place between your mother's blood stream and your blood stream and it happened when the level of what you needed was drawn out of your mother's blood stream and what you did not need was taken away by your mother's blood stream.

Your blood stream for want of a better word sucked the nutrients from your mother's blood stream and at the same time your mother's blood stream sucked the wastes from your blood stream. When one is empty of something and one is full of something, transference often takes place and I would like you to remember this for when we discuss the spiritual birth.

Mum was your delivery and pick up system, bringing you all the necessary nutrients for your daily growth and development and at the same time taking away your waste products. I suppose nothing really changed until you left home, like cooking your meals, making your bed and cleaning up after you (I was only serious).

All of this happened in the womb without you or your mum even realising it and that is because it was all pre-destined to happen by God, (or maybe a smart monkey or even some piece of green slime, or even perhaps a big bang somewhere?!).

When you were conceived in your mum's womb a plug was created in her cervix, which is called the cervical plug and it was created there to keep infection and other intruders out. This plug was designed to stay in the cervix until it was displaced by the cervix opening at the time of your journey through your mother's birth canal.

The whole of hell could have been happening on the outside of the womb while you were in there, but you were sealed in so that you <u>should have been</u> completely safe and protected from harm. I wrote and underlined the word should have been, for a very good reason, because some of you may have been the result of a failed abortion attempt and if so you are not the only ones as there are many people alive today that were the result of failed abortions. I have heard many stories of these precious little babies that were still alive and were removed from the garbage by a nurse or someone else that was in the medical room at the time of the abortion.

They were smuggled out and taken home where their little lives were restored and if you are one of these miracles, you are a living testimony of God's deliverance.

If you have had an abortion, performed abortions or were a part to play in one or a thousand abortions you can be forgiven and you need to understand that these little ones have gone straight to Heaven to be with Jesus.

I said that this chapter would challenge, stir and even anger some readers but what am I to do, just tell half truths so nobody gets set free and I write a book that is full of half truths. There is no such thing as a half truth, it is either the whole truth or it is a whole lie and on that note, there is also no such thing as a white lie, because that is also a half truth and the problem with telling white lies is that very soon you become colour blind.

God forgives <u>all</u> of our sins! If you feel you need to ask Him for forgiveness right now, please go ahead and do it and He will instantly forgive you and set you free.

I know we are talking about the natural and spiritual births, but I felt the need to say that right now and so when you are ready, let us get on with the story.

If we were meant to enter the womb during pregnancy and interfere with what God was creating I wonder why He didn't put a swinging door there instead of a cervical plug.

As the time of your birth drew near, your mother's body started to release certain hormones that would assist you in being born. A hormone by the name of progesterone was produced to protect you during pregnancy and stopped being produced when you were ready to be born.

Another hormone called oxytocin was then produced which caused contractions to take place in your mother's womb and so that you would be pushed out through her birth canal, then into your new world.

These contractions may have dramatically increased your heart rate during your birth process and may have put immense pressure on you before you were actually pushed through the birth canal, but this pressure actually strengthened you in preparation for the journey you were about to embark on.

If you were left in womb for too long you may have become very distressed and serious consequences could have followed, even your death. You also had only one way of two ways to enter this world, to leave the womb through the birth canal or through your mother's stomach in an operation known as a caesarean section.

You went through a time of being squeezed through an opening that is normally nowhere near as big as a newborn baby and this caused your appearance at birth to be distorted. Let's tell the truth, you like me looked rather ugly, sorry about that, but it is true.

Then something amazing happened when you took your first breath of this incredible new life that you had obtained. Suddenly your whole countenance began to change the very instant that you took your first breath of oxygen.

You went from being a dark blue or blue black to your now skin colour and your whole appearance was transformed almost in an instant and like most babies you probably cried your eyes out when you took your first breath of new life.

The umbilical cord that connected you to God's life development system, in other words the placenta while you lived in your mother's womb was severed either by the Doctor or perhaps by your father, as was the case with the birth of my three children. You no longer needed to live and eat in that old sack, because now you would be fed milk to help you prosper and grow.

This part of the story is going to bring you face to face with your maker and I want to encourage you to have a teachable heart because your life will take on an eternal perspective.

Your race to get here was run with purpose and destiny in your spirit because you crossed the finish line in first place and that required many sperm cells to die that you might live.

As we said before, the dead sperm cells cause a chemical reaction to take place which soften the shell of the egg so that you and your other half could become one. Someone had to die that you may live and that is exactly the same requirement that was needed for you receive eternal life, now watch this!

The Bible says that Jesus came to earth, was born of a virgin woman and then died on the cross for our sins, so that we may become one with Him and have eternal life.

In an earlier chapter we talked about universal laws remaining constant and that they have no intention of changing just because we do not believe in them or don't like them.

One law that I did not mention before was the law of sin and death which God wrote along with all the others and this law of sin and death will also remain constant whether we like it or not.

It says that the wages of sin is death, not because God wants to kill us but because when we sin we break one of His laws that he put into place when He created the heavens and the earth.

> "*[23] For the wages of sin is death, but the gift of God is eternal life in Christ Jesus our Lord.*"
> Romans 6:23

The Bible then has awesome news and actually that is what the word Gospel means, it literally means GOOD NEWS! We have looked at the following scriptures before and now we will see them in a different light.

> "*[16] For God so loved the world that he gave his one and only Son, that whoever believes in him shall not perish but have eternal life. [17] For God did not send his Son into the world to condemn the world, but to save the world through him. [18] Whoever believes in him is not condemned, but whoever does not believe stands condemned already because he has not believed in the name of God's one and only Son. [19] This is the verdict: Light has come*

into the world, but men loved darkness instead of light because their deeds were evil. ²⁰Everyone who does evil hates the light, and will not come into the light for fear that his deeds will be exposed. ²¹But whoever lives by the truth comes into the light, so that it may be seen plainly that what he has done has been done through God."
John 3:16-17

The law of sowing and reaping and the law of sin and death are the very laws that were in operation when God gave his Son Jesus to save you and me. Someone had to pay the price, obey the law and die for the sin of the world and so God sowed Himself in the person of His one and only Son Jesus.

He then operated under the law of sowing and reaping, which he also wrote and knew full well that this one would work just as all the others do.

He sowed His Son Jesus as one seed and now 2,000 years later has reaped billions and billions of sons and daughters all over the world and throughout the centuries many of whom have already been harvested into his storehouse, which is heaven.

Statistics indicate that the present number of people accepting Jesus as their Lord and Saviour is around 200,000 per day all around the world. God's harvest all started with one seed and after sowing his Son Jesus His law of multiplication took over.

God said to Adam in Genesis the very first book of the Bible, I want you subdue the earth which means to take dominion over it, be fruitful which means to be productive, get a vision, build and in other words have a good old go. He then said to increase in number, He did not say to decrease because he is a God of increase and the only thing he wants to decrease is the amount of people that have not yet accepted His Son as their Lord and Saviour.

> "*²⁶Then God said, 'Let us make man in our image, in our likeness, and let them rule over the fish of the sea and the birds of the air, over the livestock, over all the earth, and over all the creatures that move along the ground.' ²⁷So God created man in his own image, in the image of God he created him; male and female he created them. ²⁸God blessed them and said to them, 'Be fruitful and increase in number; fill the earth and subdue it. Rule over the fish of the sea and the birds of the air and over every living creature that moves on the ground.'"*
> Genesis 1:26-28

What do I mean He is a God of increase? Have you ever thought why we have thousands and thousands of varieties of fish when any good accountant would tell you that one would be sufficient (only joking accountants), or several varieties of humans, red, white, black, yellow and of course lets not forget the hairy variety in the jungles of Africa and lastly the original green slime version! (ha ha!)

Do we need pineapples, figs, strawberries, apples, of course we don't but God is an over the top God and a God of multiplication and increase.

One orange tree seed planted in an orchard will produce an orange tree, but that seed contains in it the potential to produce many millions of oranges.

The very laws that God wrote and then spoke into the universe when he created it are the very laws that God himself operates under and in fact the Bible says that He exalts His Word even above Himself.

Jesus had to die because, just like the example of sperm dying so that you would receive this <u>natural</u> life, somebody had to die so that you may have <u>eternal</u> life. The Bible says when God created Adam from the dust of the ground he breathed the breath of life into him and he became a living being.

> "*⁷The LORD God formed the man from the dust of the ground and breathed into his nostrils the breath of life, and the man became a living being.*"
> Genesis 2:7

Created from the dust of the ground that is a bit far fetched isn't it? I said before to take a sample of your skin down to a pathology lab and you will find that the same essential elements they find in your skin are also to be found in the dust of the ground.

Once again, everything you can see was created from the dust of the ground, the Jumbo Jet, the Motor Vehicle and everything else had its origin in the dust of the ground. God sowed all this potential into the earth when he created it so that we can reap what He sowed.

He sowed the ingredients to make Adam into the dust of the ground when He created the earth and then at the appropriate time, reached down into the dust of the earth and reaped what He had sowed, Adam.

The word woman literally means out of man and the woman was created when God reached into Adam's side within whom He had sowed the ingredients to make Eve and then He reaped Eve.

> "¹⁸The Lord God said, 'It is not good for the man to be alone. I will make a helper suitable for him.' ¹⁹Now the Lord God had formed out of the ground all the beasts of the field and all the birds of the air."
>
> "He brought them to the man to see what he would name them; and whatever the man called each living creature, that was its name. ²⁰ So the man gave names to all the livestock, the birds of the air and all the beasts of the field. But for Adam no suitable helper was found. ²¹So the Lord God caused the man to fall into a deep sleep; and while he was sleeping, he took one of the man's ribs and closed up the place with flesh. ²²Then the Lord God made a woman from the rib he had taken out of the man, and he brought her to the man. ²³The man said, 'This is now bone of my bones and flesh of my flesh; she shall be called woman, for she was taken out of man.' ²⁴For this reason a man will leave his father and mother and be united to his wife, and they will become one flesh."
> Genesis 2:18-24

I am so glad that God did not find a suitable helper amongst the animals He had already created before He created a woman, or else I would never had met my beautiful wife and I may have had to marry a camel! Still, I suppose because there would have been an abundance of camels, I would not have had to marry an ugly one!?

YOUR SPIRITUAL BIRTH ("BORN AGAIN")

Millions and millions of words are preached about Jesus 24 hours a day and these words the Bible says are seeds. These words are like a spiritual sperm cell because they have in them the DNA of the

Father (God) and the power to make you spiritually conceive and become pregnant with the desire to know your God.

Sexual union was designed to be a very private intimate time and when the Word of God is being preached it is also a very private and intimate time between you and Jesus.

When the Word of God is preached and the hearer's heart is open or in other words in season to receive the seed that is being sowed by the preacher the hearer will most often become pregnant with a desire to know God.

The Bible says that whenever God's Word goes forth it shall never return to Him void or empty and it will achieve that for which He sent it.

> "*^{10}As the rain and the snow come down from heaven, and do not return to it without watering the earth and making it bud and flourish, so that it yields seed for the sower and bread for the eater,*
> *^{11}so is my word that goes out from my mouth: It will not return to me empty, but will accomplish what I desire and achieve the purpose for which I sent it.*"
> Isaiah 55:10-11

You search Him out by doing what you did in the womb, you run to Him with all your might and tell Him that you need His life inside you, just like you had to run towards and search for the egg with all your might so you could get this natural life inside you.

When this has happened and you accept Jesus Christ as your Lord and Saviour you will be "Born Again", which is your spiritual birth.

The difference it will make is so profound that you will no longer see things the way you did before. Just like the life in the natural womb is totally different to the life out of the womb, there is just no comparison. When you were in the womb of your mother you were physically blind and ignorant of the life and the world that would unfold when you were born.

When you are in the spiritual womb you can feel that something is going on but you are still spiritually blind and ignorant of the Kingdom of God that will unfold to you when you are "Born Again". Going to Church does not make you a Christian or make you "Born Again", just like going to McDonalds does not make you a hamburger. The only thing that makes you "Born Again" and therefore a Christian is accepting Jesus Christ as your Lord and Saviour.

There is no such thing as a "Born Again" Christian versus any other kind of Christian, because you can't be a Christian unless you are "Born Again", because that's what a Christian means, one who is "Born Again".

This will challenge many but please read the Bible verses because I didn't say it Jesus did and he was pretty clear about it. He said no one, not just some people but no one can enter the Kingdom of God without being "Born Again".

Here are the scriptures again.

> "³*In reply Jesus declared, 'I tell you the truth, no one can see the kingdom of God unless he is born again.'* '⁴*How can a man be born when he is old?' Nicodemus asked. 'Surely he cannot enter a second time into his mother's womb to be born!'* ⁵*Jesus answered, 'I tell you the truth,*

THE KEY TO LIFE

> *no one can enter the kingdom of God unless he is born of water and the Spirit. ⁶Flesh gives birth to flesh, but the Spirit gives birth to spirit. ⁷You should not be surprised at my saying, 'You must be born again.'"*
> John 3:3-7

As soon as we are born in the natural our physical senses begin to operate. As we start to live our natural life, we become increasingly aware of the natural world around us and our natural senses begin to operate fully. Just as a baby goes from a very restricted world in the womb with less and less room to move on a daily basis and probably longing to get out of there every day, I have met many people including myself who have felt this exact same way of their life in the world.

They felt restricted, out of control, imprisoned by their circumstances, blinded by hopelessness and despair, as if there was no way out. There is a way out just as there was when you went through the birth canal of the womb into a brand new experience and a brand new world.

There is a birth canal from this natural world into the Kingdom of God, which I am going to show you as you read on. Your responsibility when you were born in the natural was not to cause the birth experience to happen but just to be prepared when the time was right to go through the experience and not to fight against it.

It is also not your responsibility to work to be "Born Again" because that is why Jesus died and it is His job. You cannot work for salvation because the Bible says that it is a free gift and you don't have to earn a free gift, you just have to receive it.

The Bible says that it is God who opens and closes the womb of a woman and therefore when the seed from the man is sown into the woman and she is in her fertility period, all things being equal she will become pregnant.

If she is not she will not become pregnant no matter how many seeds are sown and spiritual pregnancy is just like a natural pregnancy in that there is a due season, a time of conception, a time of pregnancy and then comes the time of birth.

The time of a natural human pregnancy is around nine months but a person can be spiritually pregnant for 5 minutes or 25 years before they meet with Jesus, but the principle of the new birth whether born in the natural or "Born Again" in the spiritual remains the same.

Because we live on earth we live in and are controlled by the boundaries of time, but the spirit realm is not ruled by time because it is eternal and therefore outside of time. Because of this, someone may hear the Word of God right this very second and accept Jesus as their Lord and Saviour five minutes later or it may even take 25 years, don't wait my friend, do it now!

There are many people that have had a supernatural encounter with God and have been instantly "Born Again" without ever hearing the Word of God preached. A supernatural encounter happened to Mary the mother of Jesus when she became pregnant without ever having been intimate with a man.

The Bible says Mary was of child by the Holy Spirit, not in a natural way but in a supernatural way. The Holy Spirit can also make you pregnant with many things, like the desire to know Him, a vision, a dream, a future and a destiny. When He gets involved in your life you may just be getting pregnant and giving birth to new things for the rest of your life.

> "*¹⁸This is how the birth of Jesus Christ came about: His mother Mary was pledged to be married to Joseph, but before they came together, she was found to be with child through the Holy Spirit. ¹⁹Because Joseph her husband was a righteous man and did not want to expose her to public disgrace, he had in mind to divorce her quietly. ²⁰But after he had considered this, an angel of the Lord appeared to him in a dream and said, "Joseph son of David, do not be afraid to take Mary home as your wife, because what is conceived in her is from the Holy Spirit. ²¹She will give birth to a son, and you are to give him the name Jesus, because he will save his people from their sins." ²²All this took place to fulfil what the Lord had said through the prophet:*
> '*²³The virgin will be with child and will give birth to a son, and they will call him Immanuel'—which means, 'God with us.' ²⁴When Joseph woke up, he did what the angel of the Lord had commanded him and took Mary home as his wife. ²⁵But he had no union with her until she gave birth to a son. And he gave him the name Jesus.*"
> Matthew 1:18-25

God can do whatever He wants whenever He wants as he did with the birth of Jesus. The time of spiritual pregnancy will depend on how diligently you seek Him, because the Bible says those who diligently seek Him will find Him.

Please if you don't know Him after reading this far, please don't leave it too long because you do not know the hour or the day that you may leave this earth and after you leave, it is too late.

In the natural womb if a baby is left too long they can die and be "stillborn" and if you stay too long in the spiritual womb and fight against the contractions of the Holy Spirit you to can die in the womb and spiritual death is very hard to be resuscitated from.

I had a desire to know God from when I was about 12 years old and had some Godly experiences but didn't get "Born Again" until I was really desperate to know Him, really desperate for Him to change me and set me free which was many years later. I made many weak attempts to pray and find God, but only ever in my times of depression, as soon as the depression lifted I would go back to spending my life satisfying selfish desires.

This part is unbelievable as we look at the irrefutable and amazing parallels between the natural birth and the spiritual birth that the Lord has showed me over the past seven years. We are going to follow the physical and the spiritual progression of our life from the release of the sperm seed in the natural realm, to the release of the word seed in the spiritual and then right through to us being born in the natural and then being "Born Again" in the spiritual.

THE NATURAL AND SPIRITUAL BIRTH BLUEPRINT

We have labelled each point with either the word NATURAL or the word SPIRITUAL.

NATURAL means the NATURAL BIRTH SCIENTIFIC FACTS.

SPIRITUAL means the BIBLICAL SPIRITUAL BIRTH FACTS. After you read each point under NATURAL, focus on the amazing similarity when you read the SPIRITUAL.

NATURAL
Millions of sperm released from our natural Father.

SPIRITUAL
Millions of words released from our spiritual Father.

NATURAL
Only takes one sperm released in season to make a woman pregnant.

SPIRITUAL
Only takes one word released in season to make a person spiritually pregnant.

NATURAL
Sperm had die so that conception could take place, in other words someone had to die that we could have this life.

SPIRITUAL
Jesus had to die on the cross so that we could have eternal life, He just like the sperm had to die that we might have eternal life.

NATURAL
Millions of sperm died in the womb so that one could live.

SPIRITUAL
One died in the world so that millions could live.

NATURAL
There is a yearning for the sperm to seek out the egg as has been discovered recently by the medical world. The egg releases some sort of chemical that attracts the sperm and it seems to work like

some sort of directional device that guides the sperm to the egg. When the sperm and the egg meet the DNA of the father and the DNA of the mother unite to produce a whole natural person, you and me!

SPIRITUAL
When we seek God He will come to us by His Holy Spirit and make pregnant the seed He sowed in our heart. The Bible says that "we come from the Father" and until we return to Him we will be incomplete. There is a yearning in the heart of man to know his God and therefore when we seek Him it is like a directional device signal that He sends out to guide us to Him. When God comes to us He brings His spiritual DNA with Him and only when His spiritual DNA unites with our spiritual DNA do we become a whole spiritual person.

NATURAL
When the sperm and egg unite we spend around three days in the fallopian tube before travelling to the womb where we will be in a time of preparation and readiness for our new life.

SPIRITUAL
When Jesus died on the cross He spent three days in the depths of the earth or hell and that was where He snatched the keys of death from satan in preparation for His new life as a spirit man that would occur on the third day, which was His resurrection.

NATURAL
When conception has taken place it is time for the child to travel to the womb which is the environment where they will be fed and nurtured by their mother in preparation for their new natural life.

SPIRITUAL
When conception has taken place in the heart of a person they are then in the spiritual womb which is the environment where they will be fed and nurtured by a Christian friend or the Holy Spirit in preparation for their new spiritual life.

NATURAL
The female has the womb and therefore one of her awesome responsibilities is to give birth to her natural children. She also nurtures, feeds, protects, corrects and helps them to grow.

SPIRITUAL
The Bible talks about Jesus coming back for His bride which is the Church and therefore the Church is spoken of as a female. She is the spiritual womb of Heaven and one of her responsibilities is to give birth to spiritual children ("Born Again"). She is also responsible to nurture, feed, protect, correct and help her spiritual children grow in the ways of God.

NATURAL
Our human life is in the blood and the mother's blood by natural osmosis delivers the necessary natural nutrients that her baby needs to thrive in the womb and at the same time her blood cleanses her baby and takes away its wastes.

SPIRITUAL
Our spiritual life is in the blood of Jesus, which He shed on the cross at Calvary. He exchanges by spiritual osmosis our sinful life for His sinless life. He delivers to us by His blood nutrients from Heaven and the Bible says that the blood of Jesus continually cleanses us and takes away our sin. Wow!!

NATURAL
When the time of birth arrives and the baby is about to be born, contractions begin to happen in the womb, these contractions are designed to push the child forward and down through the birth canal, into the waiting arms of the Doctor and our new life.

SPIRITUAL
When a spiritually pregnant person goes into the house of God and is touched by the preaching of God's word, the Holy Spirit moves on the person's heart with spiritual contractions. These contractions are designed to push the person down through the spiritual birth canal. When this happens in a Church building the birth canal is from the person's seat to the altar and into the waiting arms of Doctor Jesus. Many people have accepted Jesus without being in a Church building but they still must go through the spiritual birth canal to be "Born Again".

NATURAL
Sometimes the baby does not come out on its own and needs the help of a midwife or a Doctor, who may need to use forceps in order to help the baby through the birth canal to be born.

SPIRITUAL
When our Pastor finishes preaching he always invites people who are not "Born Again" to come forward and accept Jesus as their Lord and Saviour. It is not difficult to see those who are struggling with the decision to leave their seat and come forward to the altar, often, all that is required is for someone to be like a spiritual midwife and offer to walk them to the altar. They are helping them through the spiritual birth canal so they can be "Born…Again!"

NATURAL

As we have said, when the baby is eventually born they are dark blue or blue black in colour because there is no oxygen in their blood. Their face and head is often very distorted and sorry mums, they really do look ugly. I was shocked when I saw my first little girl born and actually thought to myself, what went wrong here? Amazingly as she took the first breath of this new natural life her whole countenance began to instantly change. She was crying, but as soon I spoke to her and said…. "Its alright darling daddy is here", she tilted her head to the side with her eyes looking at me and immediately stopped crying. I am aware that newborn babies cannot see but she was looking directly at me and was listening intently to my voice.

When I spoke those words to her she stopped crying immediately and then the nurses took her into a room to clean her up, but the moment they did she started crying again. I wanted to see if the first time she stopped crying was just by chance so I went into the room where she was and said the exact same words and she stopped crying again. When my daughter was in the womb, my wife and I would often place our hands on her stomach and pray and talk to her.

On other occasions I would play the piano and my wife would sing to her and our daughter would begin to kick and jump about, but as soon as we stopped she would also stop. Medical science has much evidence to suggest that children are aware of sounds from the outside while they are in the womb and so when they are born they already know their parents voices.

SPIRITUAL

I have seen many times what appears to be a dark spiritual cloud over someone who walks to the altar and also over many of the people I have had the honour to lead to Jesus outside the Church. An amazing thing happens when these people pray the prayer to accept Jesus as their Lord and Saviour. As Jesus comes into their heart and the beautiful and tangible presence of the Holy Spirit falls upon them as they take their first breath of the new life, their whole countenance changes and that dark cloud which was covering them simply evaporates away and this is the very thing that happened to me when I accepted Jesus into my life. I felt what seemed like a 100 tonnes of pain, sorrow and hurt just lift off me and I felt as light as a feather. Many people also cry just like a newborn baby does when it is born, as they are touched and overwhelmed by the beautiful presence of the Holy Spirit.

The difference between life in the womb and life in the outside world is incredible and the life we live in the world is no comparison to the life we receive when we accept Jesus. Our life in the natural womb and often in the world can be dark, cramped, dependant on someone else for provision and at times even dangerous if someone doesn't want us to be around. In the womb we were blind and even if we were able to see it was too dark in there.

The Bible says when we meet Jesus the scales of blindness are removed and we see things as they really are, our eyes are opened to the truth. It also says that "my sheep know my voice and a stranger they will not follow."

Written on the tablets of our heart is the ability to know the voice of the Father in Heaven, just as it was with my daughter knowing the voice of her father even though it was the first time she had heard my voice outside the womb.

I had an amazing heavenly experience just after I had given my life to Jesus, as one night I was travelling along a straight road in a car driven by a girl I knew. She suddenly screamed and as I looked up I saw a car on our side of the road heading straight towards us. She froze, so I leant across her, grabbed the steering wheel and tried to manoeuvre over to his side of the road, so that when we were safely past we could return to our side of the road.

As I did this he corrected his car, (we found out later that he had fallen asleep and was drunk at the wheel) which then hit us head on with such a force that it completely destroyed our car. The next thing I knew I was in a different dimension, standing and looking into what seemed like eternal blackness, in front of me were about six angel like figures that were made out of light and one of them said to me, "come with us", without thinking I said, "OK".

As I went to take a step towards them this incredible, powerful and yet beautiful voice boomed at me from all eternity, this voice for some strange reason I recognised. It said to me, "no son, you're not ready, go back" and so without even considering to ignore the voice, I immediately obeyed, then the next thing I found myself climbing out through the sunroof of the car without one single scratch on me.

The girl was trapped in the car and had several injuries including broken bones in her back. I lay awake all night in the hospital (where they kept me for observation) because of this supernatural experience that had just happened. That experience changed something inside me that night forever, but at the time I had no idea why I knew that voice and why I instantly obeyed it.

I did not know at the time that the Bible says, "My sheep know my voice and a stranger they will not follow" and so I went over and over those words until I came up with an answer. (NB: This accident happened after I was "Born Again").

If God was not ready for me to go to Heaven why were these figures that looked like angels of light calling me to come with them against God's wishes and surely if they were His angels they would only do what He instructed them to do? The Bible says that Satan comes as an angel of light and so maybe it was his fallen angels (which are called demons, and who are outlined very clearly in the Bible) trying to drag me off to hell. If I had not recognised God's voice or chose to disobey it, who knows where I might be now and so please do not ignore God's voice my special friend as He is talking to you through these pages. I have spent 7 years writing this book for you so please listen to the voice of the Holy Spirit and invite Jesus into your heart right now) that is if you haven't by now.

NATURAL
When we leave our mother's womb we no longer need the placenta that we were born in. It served its purpose while we were in the womb but now that we have entered our new life, carrying it around would be a burden and very soon we would start to smell rather badly.

The umbilical cord, that connected us to the placenta, which controlled our life, is now severed by the Doctor or maybe our father. We will now be fed milk from our mother and later on we will learn to feed ourselves. Within a week or so all that will remain of what controlled our previous life in the womb will be a scar on our belly as a memory, the umbilical cord that controlled our previous existence will simply dry up and die.

SPIRITUAL

When we leave the ways of the world we no longer need that worldly placenta that we were living in, that was maybe full of pain, sorrow, anger, violence, poor self image, hopelessness, broken relationships, drugs, sex and alcohol addiction. The Father severs the umbilical cord to the old life the very second that we enter our new life in God's awesome Kingdom. We will always remember where we came from and even have a scar or two to prove it, but very soon that umbilical cord that fed our old life will be just a memory, it too will simply dry up and die. The Bible talks about us receiving the milk of God's Word when we come to Jesus as little baby Christians and it also says, "Man does not live by bread alone, but by every word that proceeds out of the mouth of God."

When we live in the world we need natural food, but when we live in God's kingdom we also need spiritual food to sustain us and that spiritual food is found in God's Word, the Bible. So the bottom line is, if you're born once, you die a loser, if you're born twice, you die a winner.

We spoke about the movie written and directed by Mel Gibson called THE PASSION OF THE CHRIST earlier but just a quick update. My wife and I noticed that when the movie had finished almost everyone just sat there in there seats and did not want to leave the theatre. We had never seen that happen in any movie before and when I say sat there, I mean right through the credits. We saw many people crying and others just seemed stunned by the reality of what Jesus had done for them. Until I saw the movie, the fact that Jesus had sacrificed His life so that I might live always meant a lot to me, but because I was not even born at the time that He was crucified and because I never saw actually saw Him die it was difficult for me to imagine exactly what He went through.

The Bible says that all the power in Heaven belongs to Jesus, so He did not have to die and could have used the power He had been given by His Father to come down off the cross and destroy His accusers at any time He chose or He could have commanded 2,000,000 angels to do it for Him.

Jesus decided not to use the same violence that He was suffering, but to use the power and authority that belonged to Him and die on the cross. He knew that His death would overcome the Law of Sin and Death, which was the only way for you and I to receive forgiveness of our sins and gain eternal life.

He was prepared for short term pain so that we could enjoy long term gain and that right there is a great key for you to apply to your life goals and vision. John C. Maxwell said, "If you play now, you pay later, but if you pay now you can play later."

I am so thankful that Jesus did not come down off the cross, but followed through and died for our sins, because if He didn't follow through there would be no salvation, no hope, no future and no eternal life in Heaven, but because He did, you can now be born twice, and die a winner!

Jesus never ever said that He came to give us death, but He did say He came to give us life and here are His own words.

> "*⁹I am the door. If anyone enters by Me, he will be saved, and will go in and out and find pasture. ¹⁰The thief does not come except to steal, and to kill, and to destroy. I have come that they may have life, and that they may have it more abundantly.*"
> John 10:9-10

I want you to pray the prayer that is at the end of this chapter so that your life will be transformed for all eternity. When you have done that get connected to a great Bible believing Church that preaches salvation through Jesus Christ. If you are sick, Jesus died so that you can receive healing and so ask Him to heal you, or have a Pastor who believes in healing to pray for you. Millions of people are healed in the name of Jesus every day and from every kind of sickness and disease you can imagine.

THE KEY TO LIFE

Jesus is not a way to the Father, He is the way, the only way, the truth, not a truth, and He said no one, not just some, but no one comes to the Father except through Him and if we could come another way He would have said so.

The Bible says that our eyes have not seen and our ears have not heard the riches that He has in store for us. The seventy or eighty years we get here on earth cannot be compared to eternity in Heaven with Him.

It has taken me until the very last part of this book to reveal to you the title of this book, but I am pretty sure you have already worked it out.

BORN ONCE, DIE A LOSER - BORN TWICE, DIE A WINNER

JESUS IS THE KEY TO LIFE

THE KEY TO LIFE

> "*⁶Jesus answered, 'I am the way and the truth and the life. No one comes to the Father except through me. ⁷If you really knew me, you would know my Father as well. From now on, you do know him and have seen him.*"
> John 14:6-7

HOW TO BE BORN AGAIN AND RECEIVE ETERNAL LIFE

Salvation is a gift that is made available to those who repent, believe and confess that Jesus is Lord and that He died and rose from the dead to save mankind (Acts 16:31; Romans 10:9-10). This gift cannot be earned through good deeds or by simply being "good" (Ephesians 2:8 and 1Timothy 1:9). It is a matter of faith (acting out on what you believe according to God's Word concerning salvation). If you are ready to change your life, if you are seeking a peace that is found only through a personal relationship with a loving God, then get ready to be changed for eternity.

God is ready and willing to help you, right now and right where you are so please pray the following prayer.

PRAY THIS PRAYER NOW TO BE BORN AGAIN

> "*Heavenly Father, I come to You in the Name of Jesus. Your Word says, 'Whosoever shall call on the name of the Lord shall be saved' (Acts 2:21). I am calling on You. I pray and ask Jesus to come into my heart and be Lord over my life according to Romans 10:9-10. 'If thou shalt confess with thy mouth the Lord Jesus, and shalt believe in thine heart that God hath raised him from the dead, thou shalt be saved.' I do that now. I confess that Jesus is Lord, and I believe in my heart that God raised Him from the dead.*"

Congratulations! See you in Heaven!

WHY YOU SHOULD BE FILLED WITH THE HOLY SPIRIT

After you make Jesus the Lord of your life, it is the will of God that you experience the fullness of the Holy Spirit. Ephesians 5:18 says, "And be not drunk with wine, wherein is excess; but be filled with the Spirit."

It is the Holy Spirit's ministry not only to impart the nature of God to the spirit of man at salvation, but to come and live in the new creature. His job is to reveal the exact knowledge of God from the heart of the Father. A believer cannot understand, by his own spirit alone, the profound wisdom of God.

This is why Jesus said in John 14:26 that the Father would send us the Comforter to teach us "all things."

When you receive the Holy Spirit, you receive the ability of God. Acts 1:8 says, "But ye shall receive power, after that the Holy Ghost is come upon you." The word power in that verse is translated dunamis, which means ability and might. It is through the energizing force of the Holy Spirit living in us that we are transformed into effective witnesses. So, to be "Born Again" and not filled with the Spirit is like being a train without a track.

The ability you receive to pray with your spirit when you are baptized in the Holy Spirit is powerful. It edifies and builds up your spirit man and puts you in contact with the deep things of God (1 Corinthians 14:4, 2:10). It also allows you to pray God's perfect will apart from your natural understanding and aids you in interceding or praying for others (Romans 8:26-27). And according to

Jude 1:20-21, praying in the Spirit strengthens and intensifies your personal relationship with God.

HOW YOU CAN RECEIVE THE BAPTISM IN THE HOLY SPIRIT

The promise of receiving the Holy Spirit is for everyone in the Body of Christ because God gave His Spirit to the Church on the Day of Pentecost (Acts 2:32-33, 39), as a partaker of your covenant with God, however, you must individually receive what He has given you.

When you ask for the indwelling of the Holy Spirit, the Word of God promises that you shall receive. Luke 11:9-13 says: "And I say unto you, Ask, and it shall be given you; seek, and ye shall find; knock, and it shall be opened unto you. For every one that asketh receiveth; and he that seeketh findeth; and to him that knocketh it shall be opened. If a son shall ask bread of any of you that is a father, will he give him a stone? Or if he shall ask an egg, will he offer him a scorpion? If ye then, being evil, know how to give good gifts unto your children: how much more shall your heavenly Father give the Holy Spirit to them that ask him?"

In the Bible, when believers received the Holy Spirit, they began to speak in a heavenly language. Acts 2:4 says, "And they were all filled with the Holy Ghost, and began to speak with other tongues, as the Spirit gave them utterance." This is still true today. When you accept the Spirit's indwelling, your spirit will immediately have a desire to express itself in praise to God.

The Holy Spirit will give utterance through you as you give Him permission.

When you pray in tongues, you are praying in the Spirit. You are letting the Holy Spirit pray through your spirit. The Amplified Bible says in 1 Corinthians 14:14, "My spirit (by the Holy Spirit within me) prays…" Just as your native language is the voice of your mind, your prayer language is the voice of your spirit. If you desire the infilling of the Holy Spirit or if you are unsure whether you have received it, say the prayer below:

PRAY THIS PRAYER TO RECEIVE THE BAPTISM IN THE HOLY SPIRIT

Father, I am a new creature in Christ. Fill me with Your Holy Spirit to enable me to be a powerful witness of Jesus. I believe that I now receive the Holy Spirit just as the disciples did on the day of Pentecost.

BIBLE SCRIPTURES ABOUT SALVATION AND BEING "BORN AGAIN"

> "[3]*In reply Jesus declared, 'I tell you the truth, no one can see the kingdom of God unless he is born again.' '[4]How can a man be born when he is old?' Nicodemus asked. 'Surely he cannot enter a second time into his mother's womb to be born!'"*
> John 3:3-4

> "[22]*This righteousness from God comes through faith in Jesus Christ to all who believe. There is no difference, [23]for all have sinned and fall short of the glory of God, [24]and are justified freely by His grace through the redemption that came by Christ Jesus."*
> Romans 3:22-24

> "⁹*That if you confess with your mouth, 'Jesus is Lord,' and believe in your heart that God raised Him from the dead, you will be saved. ¹⁰For it is with your heart that you believe and are justified, and it is with your mouth that you confess and are saved.*"
> Romans 10:9-10

> "³¹*They replied, 'Believe in the Lord Jesus, and you will be saved—you and your household.'*"
> Acts 16:31

> "²¹*And everyone who calls on the name of the Lord will be saved.*"
> Acts 2:21

> "⁸*For it is by grace you have been saved, through faith—and this not from yourselves, it is the gift of God—⁹not by works, so that no one can boast. ¹⁰For we are God's workmanship, created in Christ Jesus to do good works, which God prepared in advance for us to do.*"
> Ephesians 2:8

BIBLE SCRIPTURES ABOUT THE BAPTISM IN THE HOLY SPIRIT

> "⁴*All of them were filled with the Holy Spirit and began to speak in other tongues as the Spirit enabled them.*"
> Acts 2:4

> "³²*God has raised this Jesus to life, and we are all witnesses of the fact. ³³Exalted to the right hand of God, he has received from the Father the promised Holy Spirit and*

has poured out what you now see and hear. ³⁴For David did not ascend to heaven, and yet he said, 'The Lord said to my Lord: "Sit at my right hand ³⁵until I make your enemies a footstool for your feet."' ³⁶Therefore let all Israel be assured of this: God has made this Jesus, whom you crucified, both Lord and Christ.' ³⁷When the people heard this, they were cut to the heart and said to Peter and the other apostles, 'Brothers, what shall we do?' ³⁸Peter replied, 'Repent and be baptized, every one of you, in the name of Jesus Christ for the forgiveness of your sins. And you will receive the gift of the Holy Spirit. ³⁹The promise is for you and your children and for all who are far off—for all whom the Lord our God will call.'"
Acts 2:32-39

"*⁹So I say to you: Ask and it will be given to you; seek and you will find; knock and the door will be opened to you. ¹⁰For everyone who asks receives; he who seeks finds; and to him who knocks, the door will be opened. ¹¹Which of you fathers, if your son asks for a fish, will give him a snake instead? ¹²Or if he asks for an egg, will give him a scorpion? ¹³If you then, though you are evil, know how to give good gifts to your children, how much more will your Father in heaven give the Holy Spirit to those who ask him!*"
Luke 11:9-13

" *¹⁴For if I pray in a tongue, my spirit prays, but my mind is unfruitful.*"
1 Corinthians 14:14

WHY YOU SHOULD BE FILLED WITH THE HOLY SPIRIT

"²⁶But the Counselor, the Holy Spirit, whom the Father will send in my name, will teach you all things and will remind you of everything I have said to you."
John 14:26

"⁸But you will receive power when the Holy Spirit comes on you; and you will be my witnesses in Jerusalem, and in all Judea and Samaria, and to the ends of the earth."
Acts 1:8

"²⁶In the same way, the Spirit helps us in our weakness. We do not know what we ought to pray for, but the Spirit himself intercedes for us with groans that words cannot express. ²⁷And he who searches our hearts knows the mind of the Spirit, because the Spirit intercedes for the saints in accordance with God's will."
Romans 8:26-27

"¹⁰…but God has revealed it to us by his Spirit."
1 Corinthians 2:10

"⁴He who speaks in a tongue edifies himself, but he who prophesies edifies the church."
1 Corinthians 14:4

"¹⁸Do not get drunk on wine, which leads to debauchery. Instead, be filled with the Spirit."
Ephesians 5:18

> "²⁰But you, dear friends, build yourselves up in your most holy faith and pray in the Holy Spirit. ²¹Keep yourselves in God's love as you wait for the mercy of our Lord Jesus Christ to bring you to eternal life."
> Jude 1:20-21

FINAL COMMENTS

Well that's it, seven years from the conception to the birth of this book and probably a week or so of reading for you.

I want to thank you for the time you set aside to spend with me through the pages of this book and whether or not you have accepted Jesus as your Lord and Saviour yet I congratulate you on reading the entire book.

I know that as you spend time with Jesus in a quiet place on a daily basis He will reveal Himself to you and continue to help and bless you. If you are not in a Church and you are able to get to one please find one that preaches salvation through Jesus Christ. If you cannot get to a Church then seek out Christians who will encourage and pray with you because they have THE KEY TO LIFE.

I will see you in Heaven if not sooner! Nigel

ABOUT THE AUTHOR - BUSINESS PROFILE

Nigel Allan is an author, sales trainer and conference speaker. ALLAN TRAINING SYSTEMS corporate mission statement is, BUILDING PEOPLE, MAKING CHAMPIONS.

Nigel commenced his selling career in the motor vehicle industry in 1972 and on 5 occasions was Australia's Number One Telephone Productivity Salesperson, he has set sales records both in sales and management that still stand after 10 years.

He became the youngest Licensed Motor Vehicle Dealer in Australia at 21 years of age and his passion to help people reach their potential saw him start his own training business, where he has been coach, sales trainer and mentor to many people including those representing some of the largest companies of there kind in the world. Ford, Mitsubishi, The Professionals, First National, Mazda, Toyota, Mercedes Benz, Hyundai, Honda, John Hughes Group of Companies, Automotive Holdings Group and Volvo to mention a few.

He is in demand internationally as a speaker and trainer at business and sales seminars and he teaches salespeople how to sell, leaders how to lead and at the same time shows them how to overcome the obstacles that may be standing in the road of their individual or corporate success.

Very real obstacles like; "I can't do it," "I will never be successful," "I can't set goals," "I don't have a dream," "I don't know how to get a vision" and on and on we could go. These obstacles are very real and have crippled many people with immense potential from achieving success.

ABOUT THE AUTHOR

Nigel can tailor keynote speeches together with sales seminars, leadership seminars and mentoring workshops to suit your individual or corporate needs. For more detailed information about booking Nigel, please email or visit our website as we will be very pleased to contact you.

ALLAN TRAINING SYSTEMS

Email: tktl@nigelallan.com   Website: www.nigelallan.com

NIGEL AND LUCY ALLAN - MINISTRY PROFILE

NIGEL ALLAN – Diploma in Christian Ministry and Biblical Studies – Ministry Training College

LUCY ALLAN – Diploma in Christian Ministry and Biblical Studies – School of Creative Arts

Nigel and Lucy both graduated after two years of full time study at Christian City Church Ministry Training College in Sydney, Australia under the leadership of Doctor Philip Pringle, President, Founder, and Senior Minister.

Nigel and Lucy are available to minister at Churches, conferences, evangelistic crusades and other outreach programs. Nigel is an evangelist and Lucy an anointed singer and worship leader. Lucy has now released her CD titled "RISE AND BE HEALED" and is currently writing a book titled "FROM THE HYATT TO HEAVEN", which she was inspired to write after collapsing in January 2001 at the Hyatt Hotel on the Gold Coast in Australia.

ABOUT THE AUTHOR

ABOUT THE AUTHOR

Nigel Allan had a childhood dream to become a New Zealand All Black Rugby Union Player. He was captain of his junior representative rugby teams and was College athletic and swimming champion. It appeared in time his dream may be realised, however due a family break up and the devastation that followed, he left home at 14 and then at 17 moved from his native New Zealand to live in Australia.

Within 4 years he became the youngest licensed motor vehicle dealer in the nation, and so it appeared he was on his way to financial and business success. Nigel's personal life however was a mess, he felt lost, abandoned and out of control. He believed that life had no real meaning because of the deep void he felt in his heart. He tried everything including drugs and alcohol to fill the void, but they only made things worse and his life was falling apart.

One night in 1983, Nigel was at Cavill Mall in Surfers Paradise on Australia's Gold Coast, waiting to go to work as security in a local night club when he heard a young man by the name of Warren O'Connor, preaching to a large crowd that had gathered. After he had had finished preaching, Warren and Nigel went and sat on the beach and Warren asked Nigel if he would like to pray and ask Jesus "THE KEY TO LIFE" to be his Lord and Saviour. Nigel said yes. They prayed together and that night Nigel's life was radically transformed. All the pain and sorrow lifted off him and he felt like a brand new man.

That was 30 years ago and now Nigel is an Evangelist and Business Conference Speaker. Not even the double lung transplant he underwent in February 2012 can slow him down or stop him from sharing Jesus "THE KEY TO LIFE" with others.

If you would like to contact Nigel please email or visit the website for other contact details.

Website: www.nigelallan.com   Email: tktl@nigelallan.com

Rise And Be Healed

An album of inspirational hymns and spiritual songs that will bring heaven to earth.

Lucy Allan had been crying out to the Lord about the painful grief that she was suffering, due to an event that happened to her when she was a teenager. She said to the Lord "If it were not for my husband, my children and my family I would want you to take me home to heaven".

The very next day, Lucy collapsed and was transported into Heaven where she found herself lying in the hand of a huge Angel, meanwhile in the hotel bathroom where she collapsed her husband and children were frantically trying to revive her. An ambulance raced to the hotel to find her waking up on the bathroom floor.

The five minutes Lucy spent in Heaven, to her seemed like five hours. The Angel said to Lucy, "Now is not your time, you must go back as people need you, but before you go you will not be needing this", and with that he put his hand into her stomach and pulled out a huge ball of grief. The ball of grief screamed as the Angel threw it into hell. During her visit to Heaven Lucy was totally healed, delivered and set free. The pain of grief has gone and all Lucy wants to do, is tell everyone about the incredible healing power of Jesus.

Order online at:
www.fatherlessministries.org

www.ingramcontent.com/pod-product-compliance
Lightning Source LLC
Chambersburg PA
CBHW071709160426
43195CB00012B/1630